JOHN DEWEY
AND
SELF-REALIZATION

ROBERT J. ROTH, S.J.
Fordham University

GREENWOOD PRESS, PUBLISHERS
WESTPORT, CONNECTICUT

Library of Congress Cataloging in Publication Data

Roth, Robert J.
John Dewey and self-realization.

Reprint of the ed. published by Prentice-Hall,
Englewood Cliffs, N. J.
Bibliography: p.
Includes index.
1. Dewey, John, 1859-1952. 2. Self-actualiza-
tion (Psychology) I. Title.
B945.D44R6 1978   171'.3   77-26178
ISBN 0-313-20088-2

IMPRIMI POTEST

John J. McGinty, S.J.
Praep. Prov. Neo Eboracensis

NIHIL OBSTAT

Rev. Joseph J. Przezdziecki, S.T.L., L.M.S., Ph.D.
Censor Deputatus

IMPRIMATUR

Reprinted with the permission of Prentice-Hall, Inc.

Reprinted in 1978 by Greenwood Press
A division of Congressional Information Service
88 Post Road West, Westport, Connecticut 06881

Library of Congress Catalog Card Number 77-26178

ISBN 0-313-20088-2

Printed in the United States of America

10 9 8 7 6 5 4 3 2

ACKNOWLEDGMENTS

The author is grateful to the publishers who have granted permission to reprint material from the following sources.

GEORGE ALLEN & UNWIN LTD.

George P. Adams and Wm. Pepperell Montague, eds., *Contemporary American Philosophy*.

BEACON PRESS

Arthur F. Bentley, *Knowing and the Known*. Copyright 1949 by the Beacon Press. John Dewey, *Reconstruction in Philosophy*.

CROSS CURRENTS

Bruno de Solages, "Christianity and Evolution."

THE JOHN DAY COMPANY, INC.

Sidney Hook, *John Dewey: An Intellectual Portrait*.

D. C. HEATH AND COMPANY

John Dewey, *How We Think*, 2nd ed. rev. Copyright 1933, 1961 by D. C. Heath and Company.

HOLT, RINEHART & WINSTON, INC.

Gordon W. Allport, *Personality: A Psychological Interpretation*. John Dewey and James H. Tufts, *Ethics*, 2nd ed. rev. John Dewey, *Human Nature and Conduct*. John Dewey, *The Influence of Darwin on Philosophy and Other Essays in Contemporary Thought*. John Dewey, *Logic: The Theory of Inquiry*. John Dewey, "The Need for a Recovery of Philosophy," *Creative Intelligence: Essays in the Pragmatic Attitude*. John Dewey, *The Public and Its Problems*.

THE JOURNAL OF PHILOSOPHY

Corliss Lamont, "New Light on Dewey's Common Faith."

LONGMANS, GREEN & CO., INC.

Essays Philosophical and Theological in Honor of William James. Courtesy of David McKay Co., Inc. William James, *The Meaning of Truth.* Courtesy of David McKay Co., Inc. Roland Dalbiez, *Psychoanalytical Method and the Doctrine of Freud,* trans. T. F. Lindsay. Courtesy of David McKay Co., Inc.

LONGMANS, GREEN & CO., LTD.

Roland Dalbiez, *Psychoanalytical Method and the Doctrine of Freud,* trans. T. F. Lindsay.

THE MACMILLAN COMPANY

John Dewey, *Democracy and Education.*

OXFORD UNIVERSITY PRESS

George R. Geiger, *John Dewey in Perspective.*

G. P. PUTNAM'S SONS

John Dewey, *Art as Experience.* John Dewey, *Individualism, Old and New.* John Dewey, *Liberalism and Social Action.* John Dewey, *The Quest for Certainty.*

RUTGERS UNIVERSITY PRESS

Merle Curti, *American Paradox: The Conflict of Thought and Action.*

CHARLES SCRIBNER'S SONS

Jerome Nathenson, *John Dewey: The Reconstruction of the Democratic Life.*

SHEED & WARD INC.

Jean Mouroux, *The Meaning of Man.* Copyright 1948 by Sheed & Ward Inc. Thomas F. O'Dea, *American Catholic Dilemma: An Inquiry into the Intellectual Life.* © 1958 by Sheed & Ward Inc.

UNIVERSITY OF CHICAGO PRESS

John Dewey, *Essays in Experimental Logic.* Copyright 1916 by the University of Chicago.

YALE UNIVERSITY PRESS

John Dewey, *A Common Faith.*

PREFACE

There are many possible avenues of approach to a thinker as original in his ideas, as varied in his interests, and as prolific in his writings as John Dewey. Personal preference will no doubt determine the approach to his thought which one will take. Students of education have long acknowledged the emphasis which Dewey placed on growth in human experience and on the educational theories and practices serving to advance such growth. What has not been as clearly recognized, however, is his wider interest in the development of human personality in other fields; namely, philosophy, psychology, art, science, politics, and social theory.

This book proposes to show that, underlying the varied human problems which were the stimuli to Dewey's thought, there was a dominant interest in human self-realization to be achieved through interaction with nature. Implicit in all his writings was the intellectual effort to work out the conditions according to which man's personality may attain its highest fulfillment. And though his influence has been felt mainly in the field of education, it would seem that future estimation of his work will depend largely on whether he has said anything significant for personal development in the fields of human endeavor which engaged his interest.

I am convinced that John Dewey has something important to say to twentieth century America and that what he says has significance for people of other countries as well. This does not mean that one need commit himself to every element of Dewey's thought. Some reservations are in order, therefore, and these will be developed later.

Grateful acknowledgment is due those to whom I am indebted for whatever good may be found in this book. Mention must first be made of Professor Robert C. Pollock whose lectures in philosophy at Fordham

University have inspired a whole generation of students and who opened for me the rich insights to be found in American philosophy. Father John W. Donohue, S.J., Professor of Education at Fordham University, has read the manuscript in its various stages of development, and his suggestions have always been judicious and timely. Mrs. Elinor Sanchez has exhibited rare skill and patience in seeing the manuscript to its final typewritten form. The library staff at Fordham University with typical generosity never failed to put needed material at my disposal. Finally, my thanks to Mr. Michael Rawitz of Prentice-Hall whose buoyant hope and confidence that the manuscript would at last see the light of day sometimes surpassed even my own.

Robert J. Roth, S.J.

Fordham University

CONTENTS

In Memory of
Walter

I THE MEANING OF DEWEY'S PHILOSOPHY

Each year thousands of American students travel to Europe. Though many are looking for recreation and entertainment, many others share the much more serious purpose of broadening their intellectual development by making personal contact, for longer or shorter periods of time, with the people of Europe and its culture—its philosophy, history, architecture, sculpture, painting, literature and music. In general they are interested in the world of ideas and the impact which ideas have made on peoples and whole nations.

In preparation for such visits, students may avail themselves of orientation courses on everything from the clothes and food to the history and cultural background of the countries to be visited. Here recognition is given to the fact that one can derive more profit from his experience if he is prepared ahead of time and knows what to look for. Such preparation is valuable in helping the student to make the most of the advantages afforded by travel and study. The supposition is rightly made that Europe has much to offer and that America itself will be richer for the varied and valuable experiences of its citizens.

Certainly no one will deny that the advantages of travel abroad are many. There is a great deal that can be profitably assimilated. No matter how much stress is given to the uniqueness of the American experience, America can never forget that its origins are European, its cultural background is European, and its future destiny is bound up with the destiny of Europe. The Old World is not so ancient that the New World cannot gain from continuous contact with the culture and traditions of the parent that gave it birth and that bequeathed to it so rich an inheritance.

But one wonders if the flow of advantages as seen in the world of

1

ideas moves in a single direction only. Though Americans are instructed regarding the advantages gained from contact with Europe, how many are aware of the precise contribution that America can make to Europe and to the world? It is doubtful whether in the minds of many there has been a sufficient formulation of this contribution. It is all too painfully true that the image of America abroad is not always a favorable one and we have suffered from it. But this is happily not a universal image. Europeans are favorably impressed by many aspects of American life. Yet even here one has the feeling that if Americans themselves were asked to state precisely the contribution which they can make, the answer would be framed mainly in terms of material advantages. The American in Europe cannot help but notice that material goods which we consider to be conveniences, if not necessities, are often looked upon as luxuries by our European brethren.

But anyone who considers the matter further would be dissatisfied, not to say disturbed, if the contribution of the civilization which he represents were limited to materialities, as important as these may be. He would like to think that his country can contribute something much more substantial which can unify the individual elements of a civilization—the ideas, the deep strivings of men, even the material advantages —and give all these things a meaning and direction. He would like to believe that there is a dominant theme, call it a "world-view," which can satisfy the hopes and longings of his own people and which can be a source of strength and direction to people of other countries who look upon it with admiration and draw on it with confidence.

We are now at the point of asking a most important question. *Does America have such a dominant theme? Has anyone even attempted to formulate one?* It is in answer to this question that the present work on the philosophy of John Dewey is written. Anyone who takes Dewey seriously becomes aware of two things; first, his philosophy is an attempt to formulate such a theme and secondly, in the eyes of Europeans, not to say of many Americans, he is the main spokesman for whatever America has to offer in the world of ideas.

Throughout his intellectual enterprise, Dewey grew more and more aware that America, like any civilization, reaches maturity only when it becomes conscious of the development it has undergone in the past and attempts to direct future development by the formulation of leading ideas. Dewey felt that America owed much to Europe for passing down a rich heritage. But it cannot merely rearrange ideas and ideals formulated for a specific culture and civilization. It must develop its own guiding principles so that it can meet the problems raised by an experience which is in many respects typically its own. Moreover, he felt that new problems which America was facing would soon become problems of the world. Hence America in developing its own philosophy would not be turning its back on Europe in a spirit of ingratitude but would be in a position to repay a debt by assisting Europe in working out problems which will soon be hers.

It will be the task of this book to discuss, in an original way I hope, the formulation which Dewey gave to a viewpoint that is to a large extent typically American. I say, in an original way, since I feel that in the past too much attention has been given to individual elements of his thought and not enough to his over-all purpose. The usual procedure is to write on his theory of knowledge, or on his theory of metaphysics, on experience, ethics, art, education, politics, society and so on. This procedure, while valuable and sometimes necessary, does not always help to give an idea of Dewey's over-all purpose. And unless this purpose is appreciated and emphasized, the study of his philosophy becomes fragmented, as must the work of any philosopher who is studied after this fashion. In addition, one will fail to appreciate the further implications even of the individual elements of his thought and thus interpretation and criticism become shallow. Lastly, such a treatment does not do justice to the significance of the philosopher's thought for our times and fails to bring out the fruitful aspects which, either with or without modification, could help to provide an answer to contemporary problems.

The present writer feels confident that there *is* a viewpoint which dominates everything that Dewey wrote and that must be grasped if his philosophy is to be fully understood. Once this viewpoint is seen, there are other elements which will come to the fore, giving dimensions to his thought which have not been adequately developed even by his most ardent disciples.

We have referred to Dewey as the main spokesman of America in the world of ideas. This appellation is justified by the wealth of his writing and by the extent of his influence both here and abroad. The titles alone of Dewey's published books and articles cover more than seventy-five pages,[1] ranging over such a wide variety of topics as Philoso-

---

[1] *The Philosophy of John Dewey,* ed. Paul Arthur Schilpp, 2nd ed. (New York: Tudor Publishing Company, 1951), pp. 611–686.

phy, Psychology, Education, Art, Science, Politics, and affairs both na-
tional and international. His teaching career spanned over fifty years
at five major American universities. His lectures and visits, made in
official and unofficial capacities, carried him to Mexico, Europe, Japan,
China and Russia.

These credentials alone should warrant a respectful hearing by anyone who wishes to gain an insight into the contribution of America.
More than that, however, is the fact that, though he is by no means the
only representative of American thought and though in the course of
the last few decades some of his theories may have been criticized and
modified, his writings contain elements which are not peculiar to Dewey
alone but which are a part of a strong American tradition, elements
which must be considered if thought in America is to develop in a
fruitful manner and gain recognition as an influential factor in the
development of civilization and culture.

The Dominant Theme of Dewey's Philosophy

The dominant theme of John Dewey's philosophy was human self-
realization achieved through interaction with nature. He saw man as
living in a world of nature and committed to nature, with his memories
and hopes, understanding and desires.[2] The success or failure of man's
career depends upon the way in which nature enters it.[3] How, then,
can man best deal with nature and above all find fulfillment in it?

Dewey's stress on man's relation to this world tends to repel many
from seriously considering his views. For those who hold for the spir-
ituality of the soul and a destiny transcending this world, such stress
seems diametrically opposed to cherished ideals. However, if one will
accept for a time Dewey's initial viewpoint and hear him out, he will
become aware of two things. First, Dewey is not proposing a "gross"
materialism. Man's tendencies and fulfillment are not limited to those
of a brute or to those of a sense-dominated human. Second, even if one
cannot agree with Dewey's position, there are elements which can, with

---

[2] John Dewey, *Art as Experience* (New York: G. P. Putnam's Sons, 1934), p.
152.

[3] *Democracy and Education: An Introduction to the Philosophy of Education*
(New York: The Macmillan Company, 1916), p. 267.

profit, be assimilated into a spiritualistic framework, indeed must be assimilated, if thought in America is to continue onward in a fruitful manner. It should also be mentioned here that we shall be using terms which will require further explanation later, for example, experience, nature, process. They are sufficiently clear for our present purpose, though later we shall explore them further and indicate their implications.

In general, for Dewey self-realization means the development of the human personality according to its capacities and energies. But he is not precise as to what that development entailed. He himself said that this would be pointed out as a weakness in his thought. But he considered it of primary importance to work out the conditions for the development of human individuality. Only then would we be able to depict more exactly the nature of this individuality.[4]

The reason for Dewey's emphasis on the conditions of man's self-realization is not hard to discern. In his opinion, past philosophies had failed precisely because they had not dealt adequately with these conditions. They had not sufficiently respected the position of man in the world. They had introduced "separations" on all levels, between man and nature, spirit and matter, soul or mind and body, knower and known, ideals and realities. Even those philosophies which showed some appreciation for the world of matter had vastly underplayed its importance. For this reason, it was man and his position in the world that preoccupied Dewey's mind and shaped the development of his thought. It was with this that he was intensely concerned. For him, any theory of man must come to terms with nature, and any system which in his opinion fails to take nature adequately into account, for that reason alone stands condemned.

If we look, then, for hints and suggestions rather than for precise formulations, we may draw together some idea as to what fulfillment of personality meant for Dewey. Starting with the biological level and applying its analysis to the higher level of man, he uses such phrases as adequate adjustment, satisfaction of needs in unison with the march of surrounding events, successful elimination of "disparity" between man and nature leading to expansion, enhancement and enrichment of the individual by closing the gap between the organism and environ-

---

[4] *Individualism Old and New* (New York: G. P. Putnam's Sons, 1930), pp. 99, 146, 148.

ment. Thus the individual is brought to an integrated, harmonious and significant development in and through the environment.[5]

Though Dewey begins with the example of the biological organism in order to explain what human fulfillment means, he is far above regarding this fulfillment as a mere satisfaction of biological or animal needs. This has already been suggested above by such terms as expansion, enhancement, enrichment. Thus he states that man deserves the richest and fullest experience possible.[6] Man has the ability to increase the meaning of every situation which is more than merely reacting to physical contacts. It is this which marks the difference between man and the brute; it is this which elevates man into the so-called ideal and spiritual realm.[7] In this consists man's happiness which is nothing less than the gradual development of man's capacities as he acts in and through nature,[8] and it is to a freer and happier future that man's activities should be directed.[9]

The achievement of fulfillment is not something that man attains through chance. There is in man a drive to this achievement which Dewey calls "desire." This term could have pejorative overtones unless it is accurately understood. For Dewey, desire means the "forward urge of living creatures." [10] This "forward urge" is something which man shares with the whole of nature and each being fulfills it in its own way. Our desires, our strivings, our ideals are as natural to man as the clothes he wears and man must exert constant effort to articulate them.[11]

Moreover, the fulfillment of human personality is not a passive process, for the individual is not entirely formed by the environment. Nor is the individual itself something static, something given, already there, as it were. Individuality means rather "initiative, inventiveness, varied resourcefulness, assumption of responsibility in choice of belief and

---

[5] See *Art as Experience*, pp. 13–15; *Logic: The Theory of Inquiry* (New York: Holt, Rinehart & Winston, Inc., 1938), chap. II; *Experience and Nature* (New York: W. W. Norton & Company, Inc., 1929), pp. 252–262.

[6] *Experience and Nature*, p. 412.

[7] *Ibid.*, p. xiii.

[8] "Intelligence and Morals," *The Influence of Darwin on Philosophy and Other Essays in Contemporary Thought* (New York: Holt, Rinehart & Winston, Inc., 1910), pp. 69–70.

[9] *Reconstruction in Philosophy*, 2nd ed. (Boston: The Beacon Press, 1948), p. 101.

[10] *Human Nature and Conduct: An Introduction to Social Psychology* (New York: Holt, Rinehart & Winston, Inc., 1922), p. 249.

[11] *Experience and Nature*, p. 418.

conduct." [12] These are not gifts, but achievements.[13] The individual is not complete, finished, but "something moving, changing, discrete, and above all initiating instead of final." [14]

Perhaps the following passage more than any other expresses what Dewey means on this point.

> Individuality is at first spontaneous and unshaped; it is a potentiality, a capacity of development. Even so, it is a unique manner of acting in and with a world of objects and persons. It is not something complete in itself, like a closet in a house or a secret drawer in a desk, filled with treasures that are waiting to be bestowed on the world. Since individuality is a distinctive way of feeling the impacts of the world and of showing a preferential bias in response to these impacts, it develops into shape and form only through interaction with actual conditions; it is no more complete in itself than is a painter's tube of paint without relation to a canvas. The work of art is the truly individual thing; and it is the result of the interaction of paint and canvas through the medium of the artist's distinctive vision and power. In its determination, the potential individuality of the artist takes on visible and enduring form. The imposition of individuality as something made in advance always gives evidence of a mannerism, not of a manner. For the latter is something original and creative; something formed in the very process of creation of other things.[15]

Dewey himself was fully aware that, in presenting human experience in terms of man's capacities and his connection with concrete environment, he was proposing something that was essential to an understanding of his whole approach to philosophy. After a chapter in which he indicts traditional philosophies for separating man from the actual conditions of his environment, he states that he will be satisfied if he can engender in the reader a respect for concrete human experience and its potentialities.[16] This text, taken in conjunction with everything

---

[12] *Reconstruction in Philosophy*, p. 194.

[13] *Ibid.*

[14] *Experience and Nature*, p. 215. See also John Dewey and James H. Tufts, *Ethics*, 2nd ed. rev. (New York: Holt, Rinehart & Winston, Inc., 1932), pp. 340–342.

[15] *Individualism Old and New*, pp. 168–169. Again: "Individuality itself is originally a potentiality and is realized only in interaction with surrounding conditions. In this process of intercourse, native capacities, which contain an element of uniqueness, are transformed and become a self. Moreover, through resistances encountered, the nature of the self is discovered. The self is both formed and brought to consciousness through interaction with environment." *Art as Experience*, pp. 281–282.

[16] *Experience and Nature*, p. 39.

else that he has written, would seem to mean that, no matter how much other elements of his thought might be revised, modified or rejected (and these he always acknowledged as possibilities), one could not dispense with man's potentialities in terms of concrete environmental conditions. This approach will help us to understand why Dewey has been so much concerned with growth. And in the light of what we have said about the process of human fulfillment as a continuing and developing one, we can understand more fully what Dewey means when he equates living with intellectual and moral growth and calls it man's dominant vocation.[17]

There is still another aspect of human experience which is important for an understanding of what fulfillment means. It is the concept of artistic or esthetic experience.[18] For the time being, it is sufficient to point out that Dewey's concept of art or esthetics is much wider than merely an appreciation of painting, sculpture, literature or music. The esthetic experience is, or can be, the characteristic of every experience.

The terms enrichment and enhancement of meaning as applied to the fulfillment of man can also be applied to Dewey's meaning of esthetic experience. In fact, one of Dewey's frequent themes is that there is a false separation between what is called ordinary experience and the fineness of art.[19] The following text points this out and also gives us hints as to what he means by esthetic experience.

> . . . limitation of fineness of art to paintings, statues, poems, songs and symphonies is conventional, or even verbal. Any activity that is productive of objects whose perception is an immediate good, and whose operation is a continual source of enjoyable perception of other events exhibits fineness of art. There are acts of all kinds that directly refresh and enlarge the spirit and that are instrumental to the production of new objects and dispositions which are in turn productive of further refinements and replenishments.[20]

Man strives constantly to rise above mere humdrum, routine existence and to find enlargement and refreshment of spirit. In fact, this is not merely an extraneous addition to man's experience but something to which his whole being is directed. For there is in man an "esthetic

---

[17] *Democracy and Education*, p. 362.

[18] This will be developed at length in Chapter III. Man's fulfillment must also be seen in terms of religious experience. But since the nature of this experience as well as its relation to esthetic experience create special problems, we shall postpone the discussion of this type of experience until Chapter VI.

[19] *Art as Experience*, chap. I; *Experience and Nature*, chap. IX.

[20] *Experience and Nature*, p. 365.

hunger," an "unconquerable impulse toward experiences enjoyable in themselves" which finds outlet in the daily environment.[21] And in speaking of economic and political conditions that can crush man's personality and drain it of its higher aspirations, Dewey says that mental poverty is more worthy of concern than material poverty.[22]

In view of these statements, it should not surprise us when we read that for Dewey "art—the mode of activity that is charged with meanings capable of immediately enjoyed possession—is the complete culmination of nature." [23] For those familiar with Dewey's concept of nature, this last is a significant statement. For in Dewey's mind, all nature is ongoing. In this process, man is on the very front edge. And it is in esthetic experience that man reaches his fulfillment.

Application in Various Fields

Once we appreciate the fact that the dominant interest of Dewey was man's fulfillment in the universe, especially as that fulfillment is found in esthetic experience, we can appreciate more fully his interest in other fields of human endeavor. Thus George Geiger has pointed out that Dewey's concern with esthetic experience is the central theme of all his thinking; a concern which Geiger calls the "reverence," the "piety" he had for the possibilities of human experience. "His educational, social, scientific, and logical contributions, technical as they can become, are all geared to this end." [24] It will be our task now to select various aspects of Dewey's thought and to show how they were dominated by his concern for man's fulfillment in the world. It is hoped that in the process our discussion will bear out the statement made earlier to the effect that Dewey was preoccupied more with working out the conditions for man's fulfillment than with giving a precise definition of that fulfillment. The first topic to be treated will be the social aspect of man.

In a chapter called "The Inclusive Philosophic Idea," [25] Dewey shows the importance of the social dimension in the development of

---

[21] *Art as Experience*, p. 6.

[22] *Individualism Old and New*, p. 130.

[23] *Experience and Nature*, p. 358.

[24] George R. Geiger, *John Dewey in Perspective* (New York: Oxford University Press, 1958), p. 20.

[25] *Philosophy and Civilization* (New York: G. P. Putnam's Sons, 1931), pp. 77–92.

things, or the importance of what he calls the "social" as philosophic category. Fundamentally this means that things can be brought to the full development of their potentialities only through interaction with other things.[26]

This principle Dewey takes to be primary and it is valid on the physical, organic and human levels. Man can develop the self fully only by entering into proper relations with others.

> The kind of self which is formed through action which is faithful to relations with others will be a fuller and broader self than one which is cultivated in isolation from or in opposition to the purposes and needs of others. In contrast, the kind of self which results from generous breadth of interest may be said alone to constitute a development and fulfillment of self, while the other way of life stunts and starves self-hood by cutting it off from connections necessary to its growth.[27]

Man's relations to others, then, are essential for the full development of the self. Egoism is avoided, however, for Dewey states that if one adopts a selfish attitude in his relationships with others and makes self-realization a conscious aim, he would probably lose sight of those very relationships which help to develop the self.[28] Man reaches his happiness through alert, sincere and lasting interest in the objects that can be shared by all and contribute to the enrichment of the lives of all.[29]

It would be a mistake, however, to suppose that Dewey's emphasis on the social group will result in the submersion of the individual in the mass.[30] He has insisted with great emphasis on the importance of the initiative and creativity of the individual.[31] He has also dissociated himself from any kind of blind conformity. For him, conformity arises when the community no longer continues the onward march toward fulfillment of personality. Thus when spontaneous sharing and communication of purpose and activity die, there arises an artificially induced uniformity of thought and sentiment which is the "symptom of an inner void." [32] Of course, one may question whether Dewey has adequately worked out the delicate balance between the individual and the social

---

[26] *Ibid.*, p. 77.
[27] *Ethics*, p. 335.
[28] *Ibid.*
[29] *Ibid.*, pp. 335–336.
[30] See *Experience and Nature*, chap. VI.
[31] This is a recurrent theme of *Individualism Old and New*. See also *Experience and Nature*, pp. 240–241.
[32] *Individualism Old and New*, p. 87.

but there can be no doubt regarding his awareness of the importance of both factors for the full development of the individual.

In any case, the important point is the fact that Dewey looks upon all social arrangements and conditions as means and agencies for creating individuals.[33] It is quite consistent with his over-all concern, therefore, that Dewey should be intensely interested in the economic and social conditions in which men live; questions of wages and economic security, of housing and slum conditions, of the de-personalization of man by the machine, of health and hygiene, of opportunities or lack of them for leisure devoted to cultural pursuits. Naturally Dewey has a deep concern and sympathy for human suffering on all levels. But it would be a mistake to isolate this concern from his over-all interest in the fulfillment of man's personality in and through human conditions or from his interest in esthetic experience in which man reaches his full development.

Two books especially bring to the fore this singleness of purpose, namely, *Individualism Old and New* and *Liberalism and Social Action.* Here one could easily allow himself to become interested exclusively in what Dewey has to say regarding early nineteenth century forms of individualism as against individualism of the twentieth century; or in his critique of rugged individualism and *laissez-faire;* or in his opinion as to how governmental control should be exerted over economic affairs in America. What he has to say on each of these points is, of course, important. But more important still is the dominating interest which guides his treatment of these themes.

If this dominating interest is not appreciated, there is danger that those who disagree with him on more specialized points will disregard everything he has to say, including his deep concern for man's human estate and the insights he gives regarding the conditions required for the full development of man's personality. The great indictment which he leveled against the social and economic conditions of his day was not merely that these conditions were dominated by an interest in private financial gain. He was more concerned with the consequences. He saw that interest in money and in material goods distracted man from that which should be his deepest concern, namely, the releasing of potentialities so that man's higher aspirations and inner spirit might find fulfillment.

[33] *Reconstruction in Philosophy,* p. 194.

Thus the social order should be a source of nourishment and direction for man's inner as well as his outer life [34] and should convert economic activities into the means of developing his higher capacities.[35] He laments the fact that the masses who labor under difficult economic conditions have little opportunity for the cultivation of esthetic experience.[36] Thus, he states:

> I can think of nothing more childishly futile, for example, than the attempt to bring "art" and esthetic enjoyment externally to the multitudes who work in the ugliest surroundings and who leave their ugly factories only to go through depressing streets to eat, sleep and carry on their domestic occupations in grimy, sordid homes. The interest of the younger generation in art and esthetic matters is a hopeful sign of the growth of culture in its narrower sense. But it will readily turn into an escape mechanism unless it develops into an alert interest in the conditions which determine the esthetic environment of the vast multitudes who now live, work and play in surroundings that perforce degrade their tastes and that unconsciously educate them into desire for any kind of enjoyment as long as it is cheap and "exciting." [37]

For the same reason, he protests against conditions under which industrial workers merely supply "hands" and have no share—imaginative, intellectual or emotional—in the physical work they do. For thousands, this division results "in a depressed body and an empty distorted mind." [38] There is also need of removing material insecurity and other obstacles that prevent multitudes from sharing in our vast cultural resources.[39]

Here we see more than a sympathy for the sufferings of the depressed. There is an interest in that which should give direction and purpose not merely to this or that condition or activity but to the whole social structure in all its aspects. Unless this is seen, one could raise the objection that conditions today are not nearly as desperate as those existing when Dewey wrote and that we can hope for a day when modern technology will solve all our ills.

Beyond the fact that there are enough social ills still crying for allevi-

---

[34] *Liberalism and Social Action* (New York: G. P. Putnam's Sons, 1935), pp. 30–31.

[35] *Ibid.*, p. 32.

[36] Recall that esthetic experience has a much wider meaning than that which is usually given to it.

[37] *Individualism Old and New*, pp. 130–131.

[38] *Ibid.*, p. 132. Cf. *Art as Experience*, pp. 260–262, 340–344.

[39] *Liberalism and Social Action*, p. 48.

ation today, the objection is shallow. Dewey would answer that the solution is not reached by removing physical misery through technology —an achievement not beyond the realm of possibility. The question is: What resources does the human spirit have in order to face life's situations so as not to be submerged by merely physical objects? Technology, too, can prevent man's development, although it need not. This aspect of Dewey's thought will be explored later, but it is mentioned here to bring out the fact that there is something deeper at stake than conditions of a physical kind, as though man's situation can be improved merely by improving his material surroundings. Dewey is looking for means of achieving through industry—and through technology, too—liberation of mind so that the mind once free may have direction and nourishment.[40]

Turning now to more specialized fields, we may begin with Logic. There are two things that are perhaps most characteristic of theories of logic. First, they seem far removed from the concrete human condition. And second, they can become highly technical and involved. Regarding the latter difficulty, Dewey's works on logic are no exception. His *Essays in Experimental Logic* and *Logic: The Theory of Inquiry* are perhaps the most technical and difficult of all his works, though his *Experience and Nature* is not far behind.

However, it is not true that Dewey's logical theories are far removed from the concrete human condition. One will be aware of this only by keeping in mind all that we have said about Dewey's interest in human experience, human fulfillment, the effort of man to derive the greatest possible meaning out of every situation. Then logic as a theory of inquiry becomes an instrument by which man may make the most fruitful connections with the world about him.

Thus in the very first line of his *Essays in Experimental Logic* he points out that the key to an understanding of the essays is found in those passages which deal with the temporal development of experience.[41] Unless this directive is kept in mind, one can easily lose his way in the long and involved work and become mired in technicalities. This explains, too, why Dewey carried on a long and vehement polemic against traditional theories of logic. In his view they failed because they fostered or furthered the alienation of man from concrete human

---

[40] *Individualism Old and New*, p. 133.
[41] *Essays in Experimental Logic* (Chicago: University of Chicago Press, 1916), p. 1. See also pp. 91, 98–101.

situations. And by this separation, they prevented him from coming to terms with the world and hindered the ongoing development of experience.

Logic, in Dewey's sense of a theory of inquiry, has a connection too with all that we have said about man's human estate. In the *Reconstruction in Philosophy,* Dewey makes his own the cry of Francis Bacon whom he greatly admired. Where are the fruits of the older logic? What has it done to remove human misery and improve social conditions? [42] Nor should the fruits of logic be limited to these details. A genuine theory of logic should also assist in the advancement of industry, agriculture and medicine.[43] A careful study of Dewey's logical works will show that with all their difficulty they never lose sight of these goals as they move steadily toward fashioning a tool for their achievement.

The same must be said for Dewey's interest in science and technology. To some, this interest is a proof that his theories will lead to the de-personalization, the de-spiritualization of man. Nothing could be further from the truth, provided again that we keep in mind all that he has said about the fulfillment of the individual, especially in its higher implications.

Dewey attempts to show the relationship between technology and the development of the self. "A new individualism [that is, the type which he envisions] can be achieved only through the controlled use of all the resources of the science and technology that have mastered the physical forces of nature."[44] Nor is the efficacy of science limited to the individual level. It will produce its effect also in the community. A new culture will arise which by the possibilities immanent in the machine and in material civilization will release the creativity latent in individuals for the making of a new society.[45]

Science, then, is not to be considered merely in regard to this or that practical application. History has shown what science can do toward achieving industrial and economic ends. Man should ask himself seriously whether science need be limited to these effects. Dewey calls for the planned use of science for social purposes; insurance, welfare, pre-

---

[42] *Reconstruction in Philosophy,* p. 34.
[43] *Ibid.,* pp. 34–35.
[44] *Individualism Old and New,* p. 93.
[45] *Ibid.,* p. 143.

ventive means of medicine and public hygiene, and in general for the relief and advancement of the human estate.[46]

More than that, Dewey stresses the value of science for the attainment of human fulfillment even when that fulfillment is considered in its higher aspect, namely, in esthetic experience. He speaks of the *cultural consequences* of science, and even of the *liberating spiritualization* attainable by science.[47] One way, though not the only way, of furthering this fulfillment is by removing fear of harm by control over the threatening forces of nature, thus leaving man free to consider how he may secure an ample and liberal life for all.[48] This is evident also from all that has been said regarding Dewey's concern for human misery.

If we turn now to Dewey's treatment of education, we find that it, too, is deeply concerned with human experience.[49] His *Experience and Education* presupposes as a basic assumption and frame of reference the organic connection between education and experience.[50] Education is the process of forming fundamental dispositions, intellectual and emotional, toward nature and one's fellow man.[51]

Dewey does not forget that the development of man in experience is an ongoing process, for he states that the dominant vocation of all humans at all times is living, which means intellectual and moral growth.[52] Education has the responsibility of forming in the young the desire to go on learning. If the impetus in this direction is weakened rather than strengthened, the pupil is robbed of native capacities and will not be able to cope with the circumstances of life.[53]

Dewey's theory of ethics or morals, too, takes as its basic assumption the development of man in and through the world.[54] It was the intensity

---

[46] "Science and Society," *Philosophy and Civilization*, pp. 320–330.

[47] *Individualism Old and New*, pp. 137–138.

[48] *The Influence of Darwin on Philosophy*, p. 58.

[49] Actually, much of Dewey's work in education was completed before he undertook to discuss in a systematic way his position regarding human fulfillment, nature, experience. However, his interest in the development of man, the fulfillment of man, in and through nature, was with him even before his more systematic works.

[50] *Experience and Education* (New York: The Macmillan Company, 1938), p. 12.

[51] *Democracy and Education*, p. 383.

[52] *Ibid.*, p. 362.

[53] *Experience and Education*, pp. 49–50.

[54] *Ethics*, p. 340; *Human Nature and Conduct*, pp. 280–294.

of this concern which led him in all areas to reject whatever in any way took leave of man's connection with nature. It led him also to reject what he called a separate body of moral rules or a separate subject matter of moral knowledge, in short, an isolated ethical science.[55] The business of morals is not to speculate on man's final end and on ultimate standards of right and wrong. In his mind, to proceed in this manner is to draw oneself further and further away from man's concrete human condition. He criticized traditional theories because, while constructing a hierarchy of goals and aims separate from this world and then deducing from them principles of right and wrong conduct, man was confronted with directives for action which were impossible because they did not sufficiently take into account the concrete human condition.

The task of morals is to organize man's desires and impulses so that there might arise a "voluntary self," a self formed by the initiative and creativity of the individual.[56] The social aspect of man is not forgotten. The self which is the concern of morals develops through interest in values that are shared by the community which will contribute to the enrichment of the lives of all.[57] Thus we see included almost all that we have said so far about the development of the self, namely, that it be achieved by inner striving and initiative under the impulse of desire for the enrichment not only of the individual but of members of the community as well.

Dewey's theory of ethics is closed to any suggestion of moral guilt for wrongdoing in the Christian sense. However he has a profound appreciation for the sense of dedication and commitment which every individual should have in furthering the ongoing process of experience and nature. Withdrawal from this involvement means the end of this process as well as the destruction of development and fulfillment both for the individual and for all members of the community. Each individual therefore has the responsibility to be true to nature by furthering its process and thus he will contribute to his own self-realization and to that of his fellow man. In an eloquent passage, he shows that the task of furthering the onward march of matter and especially of man is such a grand ideal as to call forth the dedication and commitment of every-

---

[55] *The Influence of Darwin on Philosophy*, p. 69; *Experience and Nature*, chap. X.
[56] *Ethics*, p. 336.
[57] *Ibid.*

one.[58] It is not something which should be forced by command or precept.[59] His ideal reaches its peak in the notion that each person should be ready to use his intelligence and exert his energies unselfishly for the enrichment of all.

Characteristics of Dewey's Philosophy

We are now in a position to relate all this to Dewey's notion of philosophy. Actually, in treating his concern for the development of the self and all that it implies, we have already developed his concept of philosophy. For Dewey, *philosophy is the intellectual effort to work out the conditions according to which man's personality may attain its highest fulfillment.* Notice that we have expressed it in terms of the "conditions" of fulfillment, not in terms of the precise nature of that fulfillment. As we have already mentioned, Dewey is more concerned with the former, though in the course of his work he gives us indications as to what that fulfillment means.

Since definitions do not say everything, it would be well to enlarge upon Dewey's notion of philosophy by setting down some of its characteristics. Perhaps the characteristic which in Dewey's mind is most fundamental for philosophy is its connection with civilization and culture.[60] He sees the course of civilization at any given time as a process of growth in human experience, a growth which takes place according to an inner drive toward self-realization. Man confronts concrete environmental conditions, strives to find fulfillment in them and then pushes on to new and higher fulfillments.

The task of philosophy is to formulate valid judgments about the direction which experience has taken in the past. It is a conscious articulation of the level of development which the experience of a given people has reached in its own varied and particular circumstances. But philosophy is not merely a recapitulation or a summing up; neither is it merely a record as a gathering of facts would be. In the light of past development and through the activity of imagination, man must generate leading ideas which serve as hypotheses and plans of action to direct experience in the future. Experience may then be able to reach

---

[58] *Experience and Nature,* pp. 419–420.
[59] *The Influence of Darwin on Philosophy,* p. 74.
[60] See "Philosophy and Civilization," *Philosophy and Civilization,* pp. 3–12.

the highest fulfillment possible—and man himself may achieve the highest degree of self-realization possible—in relation to the environmental conditions existing at any given time. In this sense, for Dewey *philosophy is the conscious articulation of the civilization of a people at any given time with the imaginative projection of the direction which that civilization should take in the future.*

In fulfilling this task, philosophy must keep pace with the changes in civilization and culture. This is a position consistent with the view of nature as being unstable, changing and developing. Philosophy, therefore, must take into consideration the advances made in anthropology, history of religion, literature, social institutions, industry and science. If this is done, it will keep in contact with man's real-life situations and help make his concrete experience more meaningful.

In fact, Dewey puts down as a primary test of the value of any philosophy its ability to refer its conclusions back to ordinary experience, make them more meaningful and enable our interaction with every-day situations to become more fruitful.[61] Humanity will gain by this since philosophy will be engaged in the "human clash of social purpose and aspirations" and will concern itself with "the things of experience to which men are most deeply and passionately attached." [62] Dewey maintains that common sense has come to look askance at many philosophies because of the remoteness of their conclusions from the concerns of daily life. He makes the point that philosophy has fallen upon bad times because, while available knowledge has increased in all areas, philosophy has concerned itself with a task no longer pertinent to the human situation.[63]

So essential are these points for Dewey's philosophy that it is relatively unimportant to him whether this concern be called philosophy or something else.[64] And in view of the rapid changes made in civilization during the twenty-five years after his *Reconstruction in Philosophy* first appeared, he felt that the work should rather be called *Reconstruction OF Philosophy*, which would better indicate the radical changes

---

[61] *Experience and Nature*, pp. 19–32, 411–412. See also *The Quest for Certainty: A study of the Relation of Knowledge and Action* (New York: G. P. Putnam's Sons, 1929), pp. 311–312.

[62] *Reconstruction in Philosophy*, p. 25.

[63] *Problems of Men* (New York: Philosophical Library, Inc., 1946), p. 7.

[64] *Ibid.*, p. 12.

that must be made in our concept of philosophy in order to meet changing conditions.[65]

In view of these facts, Dewey has some critical remarks to make about professional philosophers and the teaching of philosophy. Too often philosophy is viewed as something to be taught and discussed rather than as something upon which one reflects and to which he gives a personal response. It concentrates upon the history of the past, emphasizes points upon which men have disagreed while concern for contemporary problems is relegated to literature and politics.[66]

There is a function of philosophy occurring frequently in Dewey's works which does not seem to fit into any of the characteristics already discussed. That function is criticism. According to Dewey, civilization is a junction of a stubborn past and an insistent future. In this sense, current thinking may be encrusted with attitudes and beliefs which either have been shown to be false, or, if true and suited to their own day, do not pertain to the present situation. Unless these dispositions are criticized, the work of philosophy and the development of experience in a modern age cannot advance fruitfully. Thus philosophy is a critique of prejudices.[67]

Unfortunately, for many the work of criticism has an exclusively negative meaning and a critical mind is frequently looked upon as a negative mind. But Dewey is aware that criticism does not consist entirely in negation and rejection. It must include an appreciation of the positive goods of human experience,[68] otherwise one will not be able to make a sound judgment as to what must be retained and what must be rejected. Thus he also considers criticism to be appraisal of values, for only by this means will philosophy contribute to the expansion and releasing of new values for the future.

An important aspect of Dewey's philosophy is its relation to science. In fact, so important is science in his whole thought that one could get the impression that science and philosophy are synonymous. Actually, Dewey does recognize a distinction between the two. In general, we may say that philosophy is to provide leading ideas for the growth of

---

[65] *Reconstruction in Philosophy,* p. v.

[66] John Dewey, "The Need for a Recovery of Philosophy," *Creative Intelligence: Essays in the Pragmatic Attitude* (New York: Holt, Rinehart & Winston, Inc., 1917), p. 4. (With others.)

[67] *Experience and Nature,* p. 37; *Democracy and Education,* p. 384.

[68] *Experience and Nature,* p. 412.

science just as it does for the developing process of civilization as a whole. Philosophy is concerned with the ends and values for which men act. No matter how much knowledge the men of a given age may acquire, they must still have guiding principles so as to make proper use of that knowledge.[69] In this sense, philosophy gives meaning and direction to science and without the former we shall never have a great science.[70] We have already treated phases of this question when we discussed the role of science in achieving social and cultural consequences. More will be said on this subject in subsequent chapters.

In one point, however, philosophy and science seem to coincide, namely, in the formulation of hypotheses. Dewey maintains that at the beginning of new movements when man views in unique ways the development of events and attempts to project hypotheses for dealing with them, it is not easy to judge whether the hypotheses formed are the work of philosophy or of science. If we consider hypotheses in terms of applicability, a criterion for a distinction can be found. Those of philosophy have a wider range of application, are less technical and more deeply and broadly human.

> It is a case of "science" if and when its field of application is so specific, so limited, that passage into it is comparatively direct—in spite of the emotional uproar attending its appearance—as, for example, in the case of Darwin's theory. It is designated "philosophy" when its area of application is so comprehensive that it is not possible for it to pass directly into formulations of such form and content as to be serviceable in immediate conduct of specific inquiry.[71]

But science has another function which is a negative one. By observation and test it evaluates the validity of ideas inherited from the past and verifies the hypotheses or plans of action which imagination has projected into the future. The heritage of the past and the imaginative projections of the future are retained, modified or rejected in accordance with the findings of science. Thus science helps philosophy to fulfill its function of criticism.[72]

This, then, is philosophy for John Dewey. The preceding pages have assumed the modest role of presenting it in its broadest outline to be filled in and developed throughout the remaining chapters. They have

---

[69] *Problems of Men*, pp. 164–165.
[70] *Philosophy and Civilization*, p. 12.
[71] *Reconstruction in Philosophy*, p. xviii.
[72] *Philosophy and Civilization*, p. 10.

also served as an introduction to the nature of this study which is to present the over-all purpose of Dewey's philosophy and the key notions of that philosophy.

In this regard, one or two observations may be made. This book does not represent a "save Dewey" movement against those who would like to think that the decline in the influence of "progressive education" has also heralded the death of Dewey's influence and so much the better for it. Even if this were so, one still tries to salvage valuables from a sinking ship or a burning building. But if this comparison seems too harsh, it can be stated another way. The present work is not primarily concerned with Dewey's thought for its own sake, as though its every detail must be justified and accepted. In fact, the present writer is in sharp disagreement with many aspects of Dewey's thought. But it must be recognized that there are many insights which are of value and can be assimilated by those who espouse other philosophies.

This procedure may seem to contradict Dewey's own statement to the effect that other insights should be fitted into the basic Deweyan philosophy and not his insights into other philosophical systems.[73] Yet we feel justified in violating this statement. Certainly he had no qualms about pursuing such a procedure. His philosophy felt the influence of several currents of thought; Baconian scientific spirit, Hegelian sense of wholeness, Jamesian pragmatism, Darwinian evolution. It may be true that from these elements he forged a totally new system of thought—though this could be debated—but at the same time the influence of these philosophers is evident. It is only reasonable that he should allow others to follow a procedure which he found so fruitful in his own case.

Certainly philosophers of every kind have much to learn from Dewey. He, more than other Americans, had a keen appreciation for the fact that his country, while owing much to Europe, was undergoing an experience which was in many respects uniquely its own. He felt, too, that guidance for the future could be given, not by a patchwork of ideas borrowed here and there from philosophies of other times and places, but by a philosophy which was characteristically American. America stands in the front line of a world facing new problems, and at the threshold of a philosophy which more than any other feels itself a part of life

---

[73] This statement is attributed to Dewey by Sidney Hook, "Some Memories of John Dewey," *Commentary*, XIV (1952), 250.

with an obligation to enter into the events of life. That is why he made use of a bold figure in comparing the role of philosophy to that of midwifery as assumed by Socrates.[74] And yet perhaps even he was too cautious; perhaps we are really only at the stage of the pre-Socratics from whom will emerge one day a whole host of Platos and Aristotles. But now it is time to move on to a more detailed consideration of those insights which are fruitful for anyone who seriously attempts to make philosophy living, growing and pertinent for the human problems that are agonizing for an answer.

---

[74] *Problems of Men,* p. 20.

II NATURE, MAN AND EXPERIENCE

Nature and Man

We have seen, in brief form at least, the main concern of Dewey's whole philosophic enterprise. We may now ask some questions regarding the type of world with which he was dealing. Once these questions are answered, we shall be better able to understand Dewey's method of explaining how man is to achieve his self-realization, for the world he envisioned forms the *conditions* in which he expected man to develop.

The term most frequently used by Dewey when he wishes to be technical in presenting his world view is the term "nature." It has become almost sacrosanct with him since it is used in the title of one of the most technical and systematic presentations of his philosophy— that is, his *Experience and Nature*. One would expect to find in this work the most complete meaning of the term and actually this expectation is fulfilled. However, in this work he does not gather into one chapter or section a summary explanation of the meaning of the term, but rather the meaning unfolds gradually throughout the whole work.

Pulling together the various threads of his treatment into one statement, we may begin by saying that for Dewey nature includes everything that in any way comes within the grasp of the senses.[1] This would include three "categories" of objects. The first, the physical, is the world of inanimate objects which includes non-living beings in the whole universe, both terrestrial and celestial. The second category, which Dewey calls the psycho-physical, includes non-human living beings, that is,

---

[1] This is not to say that Dewey was a "sensist" of the British Empiricist school. On the contrary, he criticized many aspects of this school of sensism, especially the fragmentary character of its theory of sensation, ideas, and experience in general.

plants and animals, while the third category, the mental, includes humans.[2]

It is important to note that when Dewey speaks of "categories" or "classes" or "plateaus" of beings, he in no sense means the Aristotelian divisions into fixed classes of beings distinguished by essential differences. In fact, he rejects such categories. Instead, things are distinguished by the increasing complexity of operation and function which would mean a difference and superiority in degree rather than in kind.[3] It also means that all beings, even though they may exhibit increasing complexity of operation and for this reason may be ordered according to superiority, are strictly continuous. Dewey accepts evolution, but a type which would reject essential superiorities in the Aristotelian sense.

Three other terms are used almost as synonyms for nature. They are existence,[4] universe,[5] and things of ordinary experience.[6] A fifth term, environment, has a slightly different meaning. This word is viewed from the standpoint of the living organism and refers to objects that enter directly or indirectly into life-functions.[7]

Dewey's world view raises the interesting and important question regarding man. It is his answer to this question which is likely to cause the most serious objections to his whole philosophy. There are good reasons for these objections. For Dewey, man takes his origin from nature, is a part of nature, finds his fulfillment in nature, and ends in nature. And though he has a keen appreciation for the dignity of humanity, in the last analysis it is "but a slight and feeble thing, perhaps an episodic one, in the vast stretch of the universe."[8] Man does not include in his makeup elements that essentially transcend matter, as "mind," "soul," or "spirit" have been understood traditionally.

The key to his position on these points is his view regarding the relation of beings to things outside themselves. Objects are distinguished

---

[2] *Experience and Nature* (New York: W. W. Norton & Company, Inc., 1929), chap. VII.

[3] *Ibid.*, pp. 261–262.

[4] *Ibid.*, chap. II.

[5] *Reconstruction in Philosophy*, 2nd ed. (Boston: The Beacon Press, 1948), chap. III.

[6] *Experience and Nature*, p. iii.

[7] See *Experience and Nature*, pp. 252ff; *Art as Experience* (New York: G. P. Putnam's Sons, 1934), pp. 13ff; *Democracy and Education* (New York: The Macmillan Company, 1916), pp. 13–14.

[8] *The Public and Its Problems* (New York: Holt, Rinehart & Winston, Inc., 1927), p. 176.

by the increasing complexity of operation or "interaction" with other objects. "Mind" emerges when "body" is engaged in a wider, more complex and interdependent situation.[9] This phenomenon is found in man alone. It means that he alone can understand the meaning of past or present events and situations and that he alone can utilize them in determining and directing the course of future events and experiences.[10]

Hence, that which is most characteristic in man is his ability to control future consequences and to direct the ongoing process of nature. This point will be developed more fully later, but it is well to emphasize its importance. It is a theme to which Dewey recurs in many places and which he approaches from different angles. Thus, actions which are called mental and involve "mind" are those that include desire and purpose, resulting in direction of future consequences. Human action is by no means identical with that of inanimate objects nor even with that of the "lower" animals. It is organized in such a way that it gives rise to civilization, culture, law, fine and industrial arts, language, morals, institutions and science.[11]

Dewey, however, while admitting a difference of function and activity in man, denied emphatically a duality of essential elements. Man is not matter and spirit in the traditional sense. In fact, it is this duality, bequeathed by the Greeks to the medieval philosophers and theologians and by these to modern times, that receives the brunt of the blame in Dewey's mind for the separation of man from nature with the consequent difficulty of finding fulfillment and realization in nature, the world, the universe, matter.[12] This is the dominant problem for him and one which largely determined his view with regard to the makeup of man. Rightly or wrongly, he felt that traditional thought, with its distinction between mind and body, matter and spirit, had alienated man from the world and make it impossible for him to come to terms with the world. Unless this point is kept in mind, Dewey's treatment of man appears to be an ill-advised and ruthless attack on positions

[9] *Experience and Nature*, p. 285.

[10] *Democracy and Education*, p. 153. See also *Experience and Nature*, p. 258; *The Quest for Certainty* (New York: G. P. Putnam's Sons, 1929), pp. 228–230; *Art as Experience*, pp. 263, 273.

[11] "Body and Mind," *Philosophy and Civilization* (New York: G. P. Putnam's Sons, 1931), p. 307.

[12] *Experience and Nature*, chaps. VI–VII. See also *The Quest for Certainty*, pp. 52–73.

which have been held sacred, with the consequent reduction of man to a biological organism, or perhaps worse, to a brute animal.

Man, then, is included in nature and in large measure shares both its characteristics and its destiny. The word environment, however, needs further clarification in its application to man. As we have seen, environment pertains to objects that enter into life-functions. And since the life-functions of man are more complex and varied, so too will be the environment. It will comprise all kinds of objects, including people.[13]

Theory of Process

We come now to an aspect of Dewey's universe which in many ways is the most important and fruitful concept in his whole philosophy. It is the notion of process. One of his favorite phrases is the "ongoing character" of the universe. It conveys a meaning which is basic to his *Experience and Nature*. However, it is in his *Reconstruction in Philosophy* that it is most succinctly and summarily expressed.[14]

Dewey draws a contrast between the world of ancient and modern science. First of all, the world of ancient science is a *closed* world, both externally and internally. That is to say, in spite of an appreciation on the part of ancient and medieval scientists regarding the distance of celestial bodies from this earth, their world was cramped, restricted within definite boundaries of space and distance. Internally, the ancient world was also confined to a limited number of fixed forms and classes, distinct in quality and arranged in a graded order of superiority and inferiority. Despite its almost infinite number of individuals, the world falls into sorts, to which things belong in hierarchical order according to their nature. In such a world, development goes on, but it concerns changes which take place within a particular member of a species. Development is merely a name for predetermined movement of a living being to maturity.

In addition, the ancient and medieval world is a *fixed* world where changes go on only within immutable limits of rest and permanence and where the fixed and unmoving are higher in quality and authority than the moving and changing. Here Dewey is speaking mainly of local motion, but what is said would also apply to changes as found in

---

[13] *Experience and Nature*, p. 44. See *Democracy and Education*, chap. II.
[14] *Reconstruction in Philosophy*, chap. III. See *Experience and Nature*, pp. 48–64.

living organisms. In contrast, the world of modern science is an *open* world, both externally and internally. It is a world that stretches beyond assignable bounds, opening into an infinite space and time never imagined by ancient or medieval man, containing mysteries yet to be discovered. Moreover, biological evolution has broken the "caste system" of living organisms and has shown that living beings not only develop within a given species but also burst out of given species into new and more varied ones.

The world of modern science is also a *changing* world where change rather than fixity is a measure of "reality" and becomes significant.[15]

> The laws in which the modern man of science is interested are laws of motion, of generation and consequence. He speaks of law where the ancients spoke of kind and essence, because what he wants is a correlation of changes, an ability to detect one change occurring in correspondence with another. He does not try to define and delimit something remaining constant *in* change. He tries to describe a constant order *of* change. And while the word "constant" appears in both statements, the meaning of the word is not the same. In one case, we are dealing with something constant in *existence*, physical or metaphysical; in the other case, with something constant in *function* and operation.[16]

Extending further this notion of process, we may say that when Dewey viewed the world as onging and developing, he did not view things in isolation. The basic characteristic of things of nature is interaction. This is to say that things do not merely act; they react [17] or interact and in this interaction the onward movement of nature is carried out.[18] This phenomenon is seen to be essential to living opera-

---

[15] *Essays in Experimental Logic* (Chicago: University of Chicago Press, 1916), pp. 45–46; *Logic: The Theory of Inquiry* (New York: Holt, Rinehart & Winston, Inc., 1938), pp. 89–93. Things are "Being in the process of becoming." *Experience and Nature*, p. 123.

[16] *Reconstruction in Philosophy*, p. 61.

[17] *Experience and Nature*, p. 73.

[18] For "interaction," Dewey also uses the word "transaction." See, for example, *Experience and Nature*, p. 152; *The Public and Its Problems*, pp. 13, 16, 152. In his last book, he states that the word "transaction" expresses more clearly what is essential to the meaning of both terms, namely, an activity in which two objects mutually affect one another in such wise that they cannot adequately be understood in isolation. See John Dewey and A. F. Bentley, *Knowing and the Known* (Boston: The Beacon Press, 1949), pp. 103–118. For a discussion of these terms, see George R. Geiger, *John Dewey in Perspective* (New York: Oxford University Press, 1958), pp. 16–17. In view of the fact that for Dewey the word "interaction" always contained the essential meaning as described above and since it is the word he uses far more frequently in his major works prior to *Knowing and the Known*, it will be used exclusively in the following discussion.

tions. Organic life goes on by the interaction of the organism with the outside world, with the environment, each not statically facing each other, but interacting with one another. There is no division between subject and object, act and material. "Life denotes a function, a comprehensive activity, in which organism and environment are included." [19] The task of the organism is to maintain its equilibrium with the ongoing processes of nature. From time to time that equilibrium is disturbed and there arises in the organism the need to restore it by coming to terms with the environment. Through effort, the organism acts upon the environment and is acted upon by it. When equilibrium is reached, the organism attains satisfaction. Life becomes a series of disorientations and reintegrations with the environment, resulting in restored equilibrium, satisfaction, consummation, fulfillment.[20]

Several things should be noted. At first glance, the recovery of equilibrium would seem to mean the regaining of a static condition in relation to the environment after a temporary disorientation. But Dewey makes the point that the equilibrium in question is a *temporary, moving* equilibrium.[21] In other words, the state of satisfaction that is reached is both a term of previous activity and a starting point for subsequent activity and development.

Again, in the course of the interaction of organism and environment, both are changed. The amount and degree of change that takes place will depend on the complexity of the organism itself, or more exactly, on the complexity of its operations. In any case, it is not a mere molding of the organism by the environment, nor does the environment itself remain static in the process. There is no such thing in the living creature as mere conformity to conditions, though parasitic forms may approach this limit.[22] In other words, both the organism and the environment interact and at the same time develop. Here we see one important though limited phase of the ongoing process of nature spoken about earlier. When it includes man, the onward march is greatly accelerated not only in speed but also in complexity and perfection.

Regarding the change that takes place in the growing life of the organism, Dewey states that the recovery of equilibrium is not a mere

---

[19] *Experience and Nature*, p. 9.
[20] *Logic: The Theory of Inquiry*, p. 27; *Art as Experience*, p. 14.
[21] *Experience and Nature*, p. 245; *Art as Experience*, pp. 14, 56, 257; *Human Nature and Conduct* (New York: Holt, Rinehart & Winston, Inc., 1922), p. 252.
[22] *Reconstruction in Philosophy*, pp. 84–85.

return to a prior state, for life is enriched by overcoming successfully a state of temporary disorientation.[23]

Other terms for enrichment would be satisfaction and fulfillment.[24] The degree of this state will depend on the complexity of the organism, reaching its perfection in the human being with esthetic and religious experience.

The change in the environment, too, will depend on the complexity of the organism, reaching its highest development in man. Even here, we must distinguish the differences that will result depending on whether the human in question is primitive or modern man. Dewey has a fine passage in which he brings out the profound changes made on a wilderness by modern man and the slight difference made by primitive man.[25] With the savage, there is a maximum of conformity to given conditions with little effect on the wilderness, while modern man completely transforms it.

Another point to note is that, since the living organism is engaged in reaching equilibrium—that is, in making adequate adjustments to the environment—it cannot allow the gap between organism and environment to become too wide; otherwise the creature dies. On the other hand, if its activity is not enhanced by the temporary alienation and reintegration, the organism merely subsists.[26] The first of these alternatives is quite easy to understand but the second would seem to go against all that Dewey has said about the change and development in the organism through its interaction with the environment. The statement seems to mean that the organism merely regains a former position without development.

Actually, the solution to this difficulty seems to lie in the fact that Dewey is so much caught up by the ongoing character of nature that in his view mere subsistence would eventually lead to death. "If the organism merely repeats in the series of its own self-enclosed acts the order already given without, death speedily closes its career." [27] In other words, mere conformity to the environment without the notion of development is an impossibility, except perhaps on the low level of

---

23 *Art as Experience*, p. 14.

24 *Logic: The Theory of Inquiry*, p. 27.

25 *Reconstruction in Philosophy*, p. 85. See also *How We Think*, 2nd ed. rev. (New York: D. C. Heath & Company, 1933), pp. 18–19.

26 *Art as Experience*, p. 14.

27 *Experience and Nature*, p. 283.

parasitic life, though even here he is reluctant to concede the point.[28] Certainly he would not concede it on the higher biological and animal levels, nor in man.

Meaning of Experience

In a sense, the understanding of what interaction means on the biological and animal levels gives the key to an understanding of human experience and fulfillment. At the heart of Dewey's whole approach to human fulfillment is his supposition that man is in process with nature since he is included in nature, that as a consequence self-realization will follow lines similar to, though not identical with, those of the so-called lower organisms.

Perhaps it would be best to begin with a definition of experience as Dewey envisions it. "An experience is a product, one might almost say a by-product, of continuous and cumulative interaction of an organic self with the world." [29] Man's career and development consist in a rhythmic series of disorientations and reintegrations with the environment. If the gap between him and his surroundings becomes too great, man perishes, and here it is clear that Dewey does not mean biological death so much as human death.

Moreover, each reintegration should mean an enrichment of man, otherwise he merely subsists. As we have seen, mere subsistence will likewise mean eventual death. Again, in the interaction, both man and the environment are changed and improved. Finally, it is especially in man that experience means freshness and novelty, and the intelligent direction of future consequences.

Biological and animal life, then, form the model of human fulfillment. Yet these levels cannot be considered to be perfectly univocal. The higher the being, the more complex are the operations involved. Moreover, Dewey held that life on the biological and animal level is poles apart from human life, with its civilization, culture, law, arts, language, morals, institutions, and science.[30] As a result, the interaction of man in his environment will lead to more profound changes in both man and the environment. Similarly, in the "higher" organisms the disturb-

---

28 *Reconstruction in Philosophy*, p. 85.
29 *Art as Experience*, p. 220.
30 *Philosophy and Civilization*, p. 307.

ances become more serious and there will be needed more strenuous and often more prolongd efforts to restore equilibrium.[31] Much more will this be true of man.

Man, then, is within nature, and as such he has a tendency to make connections with nature, to recognize his continuity with nature and thus to become involved in the "ongoing sweep of interacting and changing events." [32] On the other hand, there is in man, as in other organisms, a tendency to fall out of step with the ongoing process, to become disoriented and thus to fail to maintain the moving equilibrium between himself and his environment.[33] Faced with this twofold possibility, man is unique among organisms in that he can freely choose either to play his part in this ongoing process and to follow the tendency toward integration, or to withdraw himself from it, at least regarding those activities that are distinctly human, and to follow the tendency toward disorientation.[34]

This means that man can live in the world as a member, moving along with the moving equilibrium of the world, developing in it, finding fulfillment in it, as far as the ongoing process of nature will allow.[35] In this sense, the individual is not finished, closed, complete; there is an individual still to be made; human personality unfolds and develops; an old self is put aside and a new self develops in and through its interaction with the environment.[36]

On the other hand, man may draw aside from the world and refuse to engage in the ongoing sweep of things of which he is destined to be a part. He can withdraw himself, isolate himself, arrest and stunt his growth. It is in the description of such a situation that Dewey gives some of his finest sentences.

---

[31] *Logic: The Theory of Inquiry*, p. 27.

[32] *Experience and Nature*, p. 435.

[33] *Ibid.*, p. 242.

[34] *Ibid.*

[35] *Ibid.*, p. 245.

[36] *Ibid.* Dewey also states: "Except as the outcome of arrested development, there is no such thing as a fixed, readymade, finished self. Every living self causes acts and is itself caused in return by what it does. All voluntary action is a remaking of self, since it creates new desires, instigates to new modes of endeavor, brings to light new conditions which institute new ends. Our personal identity is found in the thread of continuous development which binds together these changes. In the strictest sense, it is impossible for the self to stand still; it is becoming, and becoming for the better or the worse." *Ethics* 2nd ed. rev. (New York: Holt, Rinehart & Winston, Inc., 1932), p. 340. See also *Reconstruction in Philosophy*, pp. 193–194; *Art as Experience*, p. 281.

The human individual in his opacity of bias is in so far doomed to a blind solitariness. He hugs himself in his isolation and fights against disclosure, the give and take of communication, as for the very integrity of existence. Even communicable meanings are tinged with color of the uncommunicated; there is a quality of reserve in every publicity. Everything may be done with this irreducible uniqueness except to get rid of it. The sense of it may add a bitter loneliness to experience. It may lead to restless insatiable throwing of the self into every opportunity of external business and dissipation in order to escape from it. It may be cherished, nurtured, developed into a cultivated consolatory detachment from the affairs of life, ending in the delusion of the superiority of the private inner life to all else, or in the illusion that one can really succeed in emancipating himself in his pure inwardness from the connection with the world and society. It may express itself in elaborated schemes of self-pity and in bursts of defiant exclamation: Here I stand and cannot otherwise.[37]

Such an individual creates a gap between his desires and the things that can satisfy those desires. It will then surrender, conform, become a parasite, engaging in egotistical solitude.[38] This, indeed, is a rather grim picture and it helps us the more to understand Dewey's emphatic rejection of any system of thought which, in his opinion, cuts man off from his environment or does not help him adequately to come to terms with it.

Regarding man's reaction to his twofold tendency, namely, toward integration and disorientation, we mentioned man's free response toward one or the other. Dewey was aware, however, that a failure properly to respond had other causes. One was what he considered to be the inadequate notions handed down from the past regarding the metaphysical makeup of the universe, regarding matter, science and technology, regarding spirit and its separation of man from matter, regarding systems of knowledge and morality divorced from concrete human conditions. This accounts for his position that philosophy is criticism which will rid us of false notions preventing man from reaching full integration with the world.

Another cause would be economic and social ills which overwhelm man, which depersonalize and dehumanize him. Over these, many individuals have no control and it is the duty of the community to regain for the individual a state of living which will remove these

---

[37] *Experience and Nature,* pp. 242–243.
[38] *Ibid.*

obstacles, release human energy and potential and thus help man to reach self-realization. This explains Dewey's interest in science, politics, and social questions.

By way of conclusion to this chapter, it should be noted that much more could be said regarding Dewey's notion of process and experience. But what is set down above is sufficient to lead us into a discussion of esthetic experience in which human self-realization and fulfillment are seen in their more complete manifestations. The next chapter, therefore, will take up the important question of esthetic experience.

III MAN'S SELF-REALIZATION

Esthetic Experience

Fundamental to the understanding of Dewey's concept of esthetic experience is the realization that it is not confined to material that is of interest to the artist and art critic. Much less is it a treatment for the "esthete" who is separated from the context of daily life and experience. Assuredly, it is a theory which can be and was applied to the narrower fields of esthetics and art as we usually understand them. But it is much more than that. It is considered by some to be the climax of everything that Dewey had to say about man's fulfillment in and through nature and the focal point to which his whole philosophy is directed.

Dewey was convinced that life had meaning for man and that it was man's task to search out that meaning and make it operative in the concrete human situation. This implies that life can be worthwhile and consummatory. In fact, life is real and human only to the extent that man can say of each experience that it fulfills a truly human need; that it is an enrichment of experience and consequently of the human person —not in this or that aspect, much less as regards merely biological or animal needs, but regarding those needs and desires which are characteristic of a person. It is this kind of experience that Dewey calls "esthetic." Such a theory of esthetics is continuous with his over-all purpose of working out the conditions for self-realization. It marks the type of human integration without which man in no wise can be said to have realized himself, without which any life is stunted and frustrated.

There are two levels of Dewey's theory of esthetics and art. There is the theory expressed in the *Experience and Nature* where esthetic experience and art are looked upon as continuous with experience in general and as its necessary culmination. There is also his theory as

34

seen in *Art as Experience.* Here, too, he shows the link between his general theory of experience and that of art and the necessity of understanding them as parts of a whole. However, while in *Experience and Nature* the development of the more technical phases of esthetics and art is rudimentary and suggestive, in *Art as Experience* he passes on to specialized questions more suited to the artist and art critic. Even in this discussion, he moves so easily and naturally between general and specialized treatments that he sometimes fails to indicate which one he is handling. The reader must continually keep in mind that whatever he says about one may and should be applied to the other. If this point is missed, one also misses many fruitful insights that Dewey gives, almost by the way.

Esthetic experience. In discussing esthetic experience, we presuppose all that has been said about interaction of organism with environment, the ongoing processes of nature with its change, incompleteness, openness, and especially about human fulfillment achieved through integration with surrounding conditions. Esthetic experience is nothing more than this successful integration. It is an experience which heals the tensions set up within the individual when in the face of a disturbed situation he becomes disoriented and which fulfills the impulsions that drive on the human person.[1] It is an experience which contributes to an expanding and enriched life, which is a continual source of enjoyment, by which the spirit is refreshed and enlarged. It is an activity in which the whole creature is alive and through which he achieves a life that is enjoyable.[2]

Moreover, there is something immediate, unique and precious about an esthetic experience.[3] It has a pervasive quality about it, drawing into a unity all the varied elements of the experience. And this quality is not the result of reflection.[4] It can only be felt, immediately experienced, emotionally "intuited." " 'Parts' are discriminated, not intuited. But without the intuited enveloping quality, parts are external to one another and mechanically related."[5]

This pervasive quality makes for unity *within* experience. But there is also what we might call a unity *among* experiences. Thus there is

---

[1] *Art as Experience* (New York: G. P. Putnam's Sons, 1934), p. 162.
[2] *Ibid.*, pp. 27, 39. See also *Experience and Nature* (New York: W. W. Norton & Company, Inc., 1929), p. 365.
[3] *Experience and Nature*, p. 118.
[4] *Art as Experience*, pp. 37, 41–43, 192, 194.
[5] *Ibid.*, p. 192.

an indefinite range of context in which every experience is set; a *before* which somehow influences it and gives it its pervasive quality, and an *after* to which it will lead and for which it somehow prepares. This brings out the fact that the equilibrium which is attained after a period of disintegration is a moving, continuous equilibrium with a before and after that are more than merely temporal. It is not so much a question of a series of individual experiences as a series of focal points of one continuous experience. The experience that is the *now* is a period of brilliancy and conspicuousness among other periods of comparative obscurity and reserve in a movement that is constantly redistributing itself. " 'Consciousness,' in other words, is only a very small and shifting portion of experience." [6]

Dewey states that this aspect of experience can be very easily missed. For "we are accustomed to think of physical objects as having bounded edges," for example rocks, books, chairs, and we then carry over this way of looking at things into the experience itself.[7] On the contrary, there are no bounded edges as each experience moves on to the next. In fact, this unification goes further in an awareness that the experience belongs to an indefinite "whole," and is a part of it. Dewey insists that this sense of the including whole is implicit in *every* experience, for to be truly an experience it must have both a consummatory aspect and a sense of wholeness. In this sense, any experience may be called "esthetic," although in the experience of works of art the consummation is more pronounced and the sense of wholeness is explicit and intense.[8] Hence it is a question of *degrees* rather than of *kinds* of experience.

The following quotation is an attempt to set down, in a little more than one continuous paragraph, the idea that Dewey conveys over several pages.

> Any experience the most ordinary, has an indefinite total setting. Things, objects, are only focal points of a here and now in a whole that stretches out indefinitely. This is the qualitative "background" which is defined and made definitely conscious in particular objects and specified properties and qualities. There is something mystical associated with the word intuition, and any experience becomes mystical in the degree in which the sense, the feeling, of the unlimited envelope becomes intense—as it may do in the experience of an object of art

---

[6] *Essays in Experimental Logic* (Chicago: University of Chicago Press, 1916), p. 6.

[7] *Art as Experience,* p. 193.

[8] *Ibid.,* p. 194.

. . . For although there is a bounding horizon, it moves as we move. We are never wholly free from the sense of something that lies beyond . . . But whether the scope of vision be vast or minute, we experience it as part of a larger whole and inclusive whole, a part that now focuses our experience. We might expand the field from the narrower to the wider. But however broad the field, it is still felt as the whole; the margins shade into that indefinite expanse beyond which imagination calls the universe. This sense of the including whole implicit in ordinary experiences is rendered intense within the frame of a painting or poem . . . The sense of the extensive and underlying whole is the context of every experience and it is the essence of sanity. For the mad, the insane, thing to us is that which is torn from the common context and which stands alone and isolated, as anything must which occurs in a world totally different from ours. Without an indeterminate and undetermined setting, the material of an experience is incoherent.

A work of art elicits and accentuates this quality of being a whole and belonging to the larger, all-inclusive, whole which is the universe in which we live.[9]

There are, then, levels or degrees of experience, differing in intensity, ranging from casual experience to the intense experience connected with works of art.

It is here that Dewey's thought can be unsatisfactory for those who would wish for more precise formulations as to what constitutes esthetic experience and human fulfillment. Dewey would simply answer that no more can be said about the subject. One can use words to describe it, but descriptions tell very little. One must undergo the experience for himself. It is like attempting to explain love, joy, friendship to one who has never undergone these experiences. A person will know full well when he has reached human fulfillment. He will know it, not by signals or directives, but by an intuition which itself is a part of nature. The innermost longing of the human spirit is in the main reliable, in his opinion, just as desire and striving are for the most part reliable for organisms in general.

Dewey was well aware that both in ordinary life and in art people do go out to actions and objects which are merely "exciting," "thrilling," even cheap and vulgar. But nowhere does he imply that they have "mistaken" such objects for those that are fulfilling and consummatory. Rather he manifests an awareness that these will empty the human spirit and that those who seek them realize this, too. And certainly

---

[9] *Ibid.*, pp. 193–195.

he would say that such substitutions are a sign of the low level of culture of a given age.

Another possible source of annoyance is the fact that Dewey shies away from giving any list of actions or objects which he would consider as examples of esthetic experience. The drawing up of such a list would seem to be the simplest way of explaining what he means. But first of all, Dewey thought it more important to describe what he meant than to give examples. For even examples can be vague and ambiguous. This would be seen in an attempt to describe an experience by saying that it was like an act of love. The term love is applied to activities ranging from the highest spiritual relationship with God to the basest kind of animal act. But no one would be apt to confuse the latter type of activity with esthetic experience as Dewey describes it. Besides, the esthetic quality can be characteristic of *any* experience so long as it fulfills the requirements that he sets down. That some experiences could not possess these requirements is clear.[10] But to give examples of those that do would seem to limit overmuch the range of their applicability.

However, there are more important reasons why Dewey was reluctant to give examples or lists of esthetic experiences. First of all, there was his bias against anything that sounded like fixed norms or standards.[11] This would be to impose restrictions from without rather than to allow the course of things to grow from within. Closely allied to this was his realization that the philosophy he was proposing was tentative and searching, not fixed and complete. Hence he hesitated to propose anything that had the slightest suggestion of closing it off. This hesitancy was in keeping, too, with his concept that nature, including man, was ongoing and therefore today's fulfillment could well become tomorrow's emptiness. To set down lists or categories would be to put a stop to further development and this would be fatal to the ongoing process of man. It would create a gap between man and his environment which would eventually lead to death and destruction. In proposing his theory of esthetic experience, he felt that he had given an adequate description of that which would be valid for any age and any situation.

On the other hand, Dewey's writings are not entirely devoid of

---

[10] *Ibid.,* p. 39.

[11] For example, *Experience and Nature,* pp. 395–396; *Democracy and Education* (New York: The Macmillan Company, 1916), pp. 279–285.

examples. He would certainly respect the human values which are prized in any age; the goods of human association, friendship and love, art and knowledge, education, citizenship, growth in mind and body.[12] He was reluctant to single out any good as the *summum bonum*, the highest good, to which all others are subordinate. His only reservation was with regard to growth. Living, which means intellectual and moral growth, is the dominant vocation of all humans at all times.[13]

Artistic objects. Under "artistic objects," Dewey included the actions and objects which bring about the integration of man with his environment and are thus fulfilling of some human drive. This is true whether the objects in question are those of daily experience or those which are ordinarily termed "artistic" in the technical sense.

In any case, Dewey maintains that there is an unfortunate division between the general and specialized meaning of artistic objects. As a result, art in the technical sense is now confined to the art gallery and library, and we have the strange situation where people must go to such places in order to enjoy an "esthetic" experience. But this was not always so. Paintings, buildings, statues, language, pottery, even table utensils, were ornamented to enhance daily living and were not separated from it or put aside for the appreciative gaze of an elite.[14] They were formed and used by people who had undergone an enriched experience and who could not be content until that experience was given expression in some outward way. That such a procedure has disappeared from contemporary life is to be regretted and tells a tale regarding the level of human development of a given age.[15] It is this division which Dewey is anxious to remove by his theory of esthetics.

Artist. Similarly, Dewey would want to remove the hard and fast division between the "artist" and the ordinary person. In a real sense, every human being is an artist in that he has the capacity to create consummatory objects and actions and in the process to create his own individuality and personality and those of others.[16] The artist is distinguished from ordinary people by the fact that he is unusually sensi-

---

12 *A Common Faith* (New Haven: Yale University Press, 1934), pp. 48, 51, 56, 71.

13 *Democracy and Education*, p. 362.

14 *Art as Experience*, p. 261.

15 *Ibid.*, pp. 53–54.

16 See *Individualism Old and New* (New York: G. P. Putnam's Sons, 1930), pp. 168–169; *Art as Experience*, pp. 281–282.

tive to the qualities of things and has at his command the powers of execution so as to express his innermost self in ways that are called "artistic." [17] But since everyone is in a true sense an artist by reason of the fact that he is human, there is reason to hope that everyone will heighten the degree of his esthetic experience as well as the degree of artistry in the things and actions that he produces. In fact, growth in human fulfillment suitable to each age depends on it. It is the rigid division which makes it difficult for the strict artist to find integration in his environment, since he is looked upon as eccentric, out of step with daily life and hence is an object of misunderstanding, if not of ridicule, to his contemporaries.[18]

Art. Art, too, has various levels of meaning. As a beginning, Dewey goes back to the Greek concept of experience and shows its link with art.

> Experience, with the Greeks, signified a store of practical wisdom, a fund of insights useful in conducting the affairs of life. Sensation and perception were its occasion and supplied it with pertinent materials, but did not of themselves constitute it. They generated experience when retention was added and when a common factor in the multitude of felt and perceived cases detached itself so as to become available to judgment and exertion. Thus understood, experience is exemplified in the discrimination and skill of the good carpenter, pilot, physician, captain-at-arms; experience is equivalent to art.[19]

Though Dewey criticized many other aspects of Greek thought, he accepted this aspect as fundamental to his whole theory of art. For him, experience, art, consisted in *making* and *doing*. He thus describes it in this, its widest sense.

> Every art does something with some physical material, the body or something outside the body, with or without the use of intervening tools, and with a view to production of something visible, audible, or tangible.[20]

From this point of view, art could apply to any form of production.

Dewey then shows the connection between art as production and esthetic experience. In this sense, "art is a process of production in

---

[17] *Art as Experience*, p. 49.

[18] *Ibid.*, p. 9. See also *Individualism Old and New*, p. 40. Dewey also recognized that the fault may be found in the artist. See *Experience and Nature*, p. 363; *Art as Experience*, p. 9.

[19] *Experience and Nature*, p. 354.

[20] *Art as Experience*, p. 47.

which natural materials are re-shaped in a projection toward consummatory fulfillment through regulation of trains of events that occur in a less regulated way on lower levels of nature." [21] It is through art that the human being in seeking integration with his environment does not have to wait until external conditions arrange themselves adequately.[22] In a sense, no organism in its interaction does merely that. It could do so occasionally, for in Dewey's opinion nature does provide situations which are inherently satisfying. However, all organisms go out in some way to meet the environment and to interact with it. Man can do more in deliberately arranging the course of events either to repeat conditions that have led to a consummatory experience in the past or actually to rearrange and reshape conditions so that they may be productive of new experiences and new consummations. In either case, art is now seen as related to consummatory experience and therefore to man's self-realization in and through matter.

For Dewey, it is art that distinguishes man from the rest of nature.[23] He alone of all beings in nature can use his intelligence to discover the secret connecting links in nature, to recombine them and thus to control the course of future events, the course of future consummatory experiences. When the idea of art became a conscious idea, the history of humanity reached its greatest intellectual achievement and the possibility of invention of new arts, along with the use of old ones, became the guiding ideal of mankind.[24]

But if art raises man above all other beings of nature, it also ties him to nature.[25] For in the exercise of art, man must act in accordance with the structure of his organism: brain, sense-organs and muscular system. And like any organic activity, art is possible only by interaction with environment. It is only in and through nature that man can exercise art and thus achieve his self-realization. Thus we see that art at once distinguishes man from the rest of nature and binds him more closely to it.

From another point of view, it is by reason of this close connection of man with nature in art that nature itself may be said to be enhanced.

---

[21] *Experience and Nature,* p. viii.

[22] *Ibid.,* p. 372.

[23] *Art as Experience,* p. 26.

[24] *Ibid.*

[25] *Ibid.,* pp. 25–26. See also *The Public and Its Problems* (New York: Holt, Rinehart & Winston, Inc., 1927), p. 8.

For if man is included in nature, and if it is art that gives man his high status, then in a sense we may say that in art, nature itself reaches its high point. In fact, Dewey states that art represents the culminating event of nature as well as the climax of experience.[26] Man may then be seen to be spearheading the ongoing process of nature and, in fact, directing the future course of that process.

Only a brief remark need be made of art in its technical sense. This obviously refers to the activity of the artist as he fashions objects which we ordinarily call "works of art" and which, in contemporary society at least, are unfortunately reserved for the museum and art gallery. It should also be recalled that the principles set down by Dewey regarding art apply almost without change to art both in daily life and in its technical sense.

Means and Ends—Instrumental and Consummatory

Dewey has now reached the point where esthetic experience is seen to constitute man's self-realization. He has also shown that these are not confined to special categories of experience. From this point of view, he has saved "ordinary" experience from being exiled outside the scope of human fulfillment and he has also shown that the dull and uninspired need not be the "ordinary" thing.

But what about the opposite extreme? Does the "ordinary" now become the fulfilling such that in *every* experience man may reach completion and satisfaction? Everyone is aware that some activities are not inherently or immediately enjoyable.[27] This is clear to anyone who has labored long and tediously over a term paper, a business transaction, a recalcitrant machine or a stubborn lawn. In no wise would we call them inherently consummatory in the sense in which that term has been used thus far. What are we to say about such operations? Are they beyond the power of redemption, beyond the scope and meaning of self-realization? Do they stand off and mock us with the reminder that no matter how much we may talk about and strive for experiences that are consummatory, they will sooner or later enter into our lives as an intolerable burden? Must our lives be

---

26 *Experience and Nature,* p. ix.
27 *Ibid.,* p. 362.

departmentalized into actions that are satisfying and inspiring, and those that are frustrating and deadening? These are important questions, for actions of the latter type comprise a large part of one's daily life.

Dewey attempts to answer this vexing problem by showing the relation of means and consequence, process and product, instrumental and consummatory.[28] A large part of his theory of art has for its purpose to show that art itself is any activity which is simultaneously both, and that "normal artistic experience involves bringing to a better balance than is found elsewhere in either nature or experience the consummatory and instrumental phases of events." [29] In other words, an activity that is truly artistic, truly esthetic, and therefore truly meaningful for man, must in some way be both instrumental and consummatory, even though not every activity will possess these two characteristics in the same degree.

Let us begin with an experience which is inherently satisfying. It represents the successful completion of actions following upon a disturbed situation. Man has regained his integration with the ongoing series of events. Such an experience would seem to be one to which other experiences are directed, in which, in fact, the other activities find their meaning and completion. In what sense can the consummatory experience be said to be instrumental?

Dewey's concept of fulfillment as a moving equilibrium gives the key to the solution. This has been treated before and it is basic to the whole development of Dewey's thought.[30] Equilibrium is both a term of previous experiences as well as a starting point for a further one. The experience of the present moment is what it is by reason of previous activities through which it has been created and shaped. Likewise, what it is now will determine the nature of future experiences, for it carries into them the whole of its past. All this follows, too, from the concept of nature as pushing forward so that each present moment is a poising for the next, each experience a future implicated in a present.

Applying this to our present problem, Dewey states:

> There are acts of all kinds that directly refresh and enlarge the spirit and that are instrumental to the production of new objects and disposi-

---

[28] *Ibid.*, p. 361.
[29] *Ibid.*, pp. viii–ix.
[30] *Supra,* chap. II.

tions which are in turn productive of further refinements and replenishments.[31]

Each consummatory experience quickens and heightens our power of apprehension, enlarges our vision, refines our powers of discrimination and creates standards of apprehension so that we are better able to grasp the meaning of future situations.[32]

In *Art as Experience*, Dewey develops the same point in connection with the appreciation of a work of art,[33] and though he is discussing art in its technical aspects, what he says applies as well to ordinary experience. He also explicitly shows how the consummatory experience of a work of art is instrumental for ordinary experience when he states that by a work of art "we are carried to a refreshed attitude toward the circumstances and exigencies of ordinary experience." [34] Its efficacy continues indirectly in that we carry back to ordinary experience an enduring serenity, refreshment and re-education of vision.

The instrumental aspect of art is essential not only to the theory of art itself but to the whole concept of experience as ongoing. For, unless the consummatory experience is indefinitely instrumental to new satisfying events, the individual reaches satiety and the experience turns into boredom.[35] This would be fatal, for the whole onward movement would grind to a halt and the cessation of consummatory or integrating experience would introduce a gap between man and his environment. This would mean the end of man's self-realization.

Let us now turn to experiences which are *not* inherently consummatory but which may lead to one that is. Examples of such activities would be: study in order to attain a degree, research in order to develop a medicine, labor in order to earn a living, hospitalization in order to regain health. The instrumental aspect of these activities is clear. In fact, the exaggeration of it to the exclusion of any other is precisely the thing that creates the problem. It is the consummatory aspect that requires an explanation. The solution lies in the possession and appreciation of the meaning of things.[36] This is another way of saying that man must first be aware of his over-all purpose which is self-

---

31 *Experience and Nature*, p. 365.
32 *Ibid.*, p. 366.
33 *Art as Experience*, p. 139.
34 *Ibid.*
35 *Experience and Nature*, p. 365.
36 *Ibid.*, p. 362.

realization through the achievement of consummatory experience. It is this experience which constitutes the good and reasonable life,[37] a life which is truly human and rational.[38] It is this kind of experience which here as in every aspect of Dewey's concept of experience holds a commanding position.

And to be a truly rational and human life, this consummatory experience must be consciously possessed and appreciated by the individual such that it must be deliberately chosen as the goal of all his striving. Further, the individual must consciously and deliberately choose the steps to be taken in order that this experience may be achieved. In other words, he must *freely* avail himself of certain conditions because of *perceived* connection with *chosen* consequences.[39] In fact, it is this which distinguishes man from the animal.[40]

Notice what Dewey is attempting to do. With consummatory experience as central, he is attempting to show how its influence can and must radiate outward so as to include as many actions as possible within its glow. Just as objects receive less light as their distance from the source increases, so here we notice degrees to which activities share in the influence of the consummatory experience.

This is clear in the examples which Dewey gives to illustrate his point. There are some objects in which the material used in production enters very intimately into the object. This is true of works of art. "Colors *are* the painting; tones are the music." [41] The material may be called "means," if we wish, but there is a distinction between a *mere* means which is external to the thing produced, and a *medium*, the kind of means which is "taken up into the consequences produced and remains immanent in them." [42] In this sense, color, tone, clay, language, would be *media*. To illustrate his point further, Dewey also gives examples of baking bread where flour, water, yeast are means of bread because they are ingredients of bread; and of building where brick and mortar become part of the house which they are used to build.[43]

The distinction between means and medium is clear enough in the

37 *Ibid.*, p. 367.
38 *Ibid.*, p. 369.
39 *Ibid.*, p. 366.
40 *Ibid.*, pp. 368–371.
41 *Art as Experience*, p. 197. See *Experience and Nature*, p. 367.
42 *Art as Experience*, p. 197.
43 *Ibid.*

examples given, for quite obviously the materials used enter into the makeup of the thing produced. But can *every* means be called a medium in the sense used by Dewey? If so, it would have to enter into the composition of the product. And yet, we can easily think of many cases where the connection between means and end is much less close; for example, labor as a means for earning a living, the consulting of a physician in order to recover health, the conducting of a campaign in order to gain a political position. These means would seem to be entirely external to what is accomplished and so would seem to be reduced to the status of *mere* means.

But it is quite clear that Dewey intends to eliminate the distinction between mere means and medium even in these cases, no matter what common usage implies. For, in speaking of art, he gives examples which are not as clear as color and tone; for example, susceptibility of ear as a means of music,[44] and in painting, brush-strokes,[45] skill of the artist,[46] rhythm or the organization of energies.[47] These, he maintains, must not remain external to the object but must become part of the work produced. He shows the same extension of meaning when he speaks of the things of ordinary life. "A good political constitution, honest police-system, and competent judiciary, are means of the prosperous life of the community because they are integrated portions of that life." [48]

What Dewey intends here is that every means *can* be a medium, provided that it is seen in its proper light, that is, as consciously related to consummatory experience, to self-realization. This is the full meaning of his statement to the effect that a means is that which is *freely* used because of *perceived* connection with *chosen* consequences. When a means is seen in relation to its end, it is put into a different context, it is raised to a new status and becomes the object of special attention. We give it the same love and care that we give to the end.[49] The end by its abiding presence breathes meaning, spirit and life into those acts and objects which bring about the achievement of the goal.

In all this, however, Dewey is not naïve enough to suppose that his

---

44 *Experience and Nature*, p. 367.
45 *Art as Experience*, p. 199.
46 *Ibid.*, p. 140.
47 *Ibid.*, p. 170.
48 *Experience and Nature*, p. 367.
49 *Ibid.*, pp. 366–367.

position regarding the consummatory and instrumental will take the labor and hardship out of existence. The proper view of means as medium through its relation to a consummatory experience will not necessarily make the medium itself consummatory in the full sense. Of course, the medium may be consummatory in its own right. An advertisement in its praise of a well-known automobile will assure us that "the fun is in the going." But this is not always the case. Besides, there are frustrations and disorientations in life. This is the whole burden of the second chapter of *Experience and Nature*. In fact, it is these experiences that make consummatory experiences possible. If all experiences were consummatory, life would turn to boredom. No, Dewey is quite aware that the achievement of self-realization entails hard work. But certainly his theory will give meaning and dignity to many aspects of life, making them worthwhile. And who can deny that when hard work is seen in its relation to a goal, it, too, is quickened and assumes at least a modicum of satisfaction.

With this, the discussion of self-realization as seen in esthetic experience comes to a close. It will be the task of the next two chapters to discuss self-realization as it confronts modern industry and science.

IV   TECHNOLOGY AND SELF-REALIZATION

Since science and technology had such an important place in Dewey's work, any discussion of his thought must confront these problems. Dewey saw that man's integration in the civilization in which we live must take into consideration the role of science. It forms so much a part of man's life that it cannot be ignored. "Science is here," he states, "and a new integration must take account of it and include it."[1] He was also conscious of the fact that, in the minds of many, science was the chief obstacle to any satisfactory attempt to work out man's fulfillment. On many occasions he stated that science has become the scapegoat for all that is disruptive of man's development as a person and for all that tends to depersonalize and mechanize him. Unless he can adequately deal with science, the task of working out the conditions for man's self-realization will remain incomplete, or rather will be entirely vitiated.

Dewey confronted the task with vigor and decision. He attempted to show that science is not aligned against man. And he did this not by showing how man can merely tolerate science by making an uneasy truce with it. His plan was not to neutralize its evil effects so that man would store up spiritual energy, vaccinate himself, as it were, so that he might return to deal it without being infected. He was convinced that "science is made by man for man,"[2] and we know what he meant by man in terms of his highest fulfillment. And if it is made for man, instead of meaning all that is detrimental to man's development, it is rather that through which man must attain his self-realization.

---

[1] *Art as Experience* (New York: G. P. Putnam's Sons, 1934), p. 341.

[2] *Experience and Nature* (New York: W. W. Norton & Company, Inc., 1929), p. 382.

As soon as we begin to discuss Dewey's position on science we are faced with a difficulty in terminology. He uses the term "science" in both a generic and specific sense. In addition, he will sometimes shift from one meaning to the other without warning. At one moment, science is a more generic term which includes logic, reflection, reflective inquiry (or merely inquiry), thought, intelligence, mind, reason, and sometimes knowledge. At another moment, science will assume the modern connotation of the physical sciences, for example, physics and chemistry, or science as it is applied in industry and which goes by the name of technology.

It is possible, however, to separate the two meanings of the term with their synonyms and subdivisions. On the one hand, science stands for a general method or tool of inquiry and, on the other, it means this general method as it assumes instruments and techniques of experimentation, whether this occurs in industry and then goes by the name of technology, or as it occurs in the "natural sciences" such as biology, physics, chemistry.[3] Perhaps Dewey has given his clearest explanation when he classifies the first as "scientific temper" and the second as "scientific technique."[4]

In any case, we know what science is *not*, in Dewey's opinion. It is not a kind of knowledge which grasps the permanent, the abiding, the real, as opposed to a type of knowledge which deals merely with the changing, the ephemeral, the apparent. Furthermore, it is *doing*, as opposed to idle contemplation. It does not separate man from nature but it is that through which man enters into nature and into its on-going processes. Lastly, it is not that which merely mirrors reality but that which actually controls it and determines its subsequent course of development.

In view of the varied aspects of science, one becomes puzzled as to just where to begin. A decision must be made regarding the order of treatment and, in this instance, the choice is dictated by Dewey's main concern which is man's self-realization. With this in mind, we

---

[3] Even this division is not rigid. For example, where would one put medicine, or experimental psychology, or some of the social sciences, as anthropology, sociology? Some of these take on the techniques of natural sciences. See *Experience and Nature*, pp. 162–165; *Knowing and the Known* (Boston: The Beacon Press, 1949), p. 279. However, if we use the criterion of experiments under laboratory conditions as that which makes the discipline science in the second of the above senses, we shall avoid endless and needless quibbling.

[4] *Problems of Men* (New York: Philosophical Library, Inc., 1946), p. 173.

shall begin with a discussion of modern technology since it was this phase of science that engaged so much of Dewey's attention.

Technology

As a starting point, it seems necessary to accept the premise that the continued development of technology is inevitable. This has been admitted even by those who would point out its dangers.[5] It is neither an argument in favor of technology nor a pessimistic and reluctant acceptance of it, as if one were to say that there is no sense in preaching charity or justice since people are going to be uncharitable and unjust anyway. More important than this inevitability is the reason behind such a condition.

One approach has been to see the current rise in technology as a phase of evolutionary development. Walter Ong has proposed this view with enthusiasm. For him, the technological age cannot be understood except as an epoch in a totality of evolution, cosmic, intellectual and social, and an epoch which is keenly conscious of its own place in the total process. It is a shape which material reality takes at a certain stage of its development for which preceding ages have prepared over a long period of time and these in turn develop into something else.

> For this age is most strikingly something which has not existed before and yet something into which the preceding history of human society and of human thought has led, as well as something pregnant with a future sure to be different from both present and past.[6]

This viewpoint opens wider and clearer perspectives from which to consider technology. It reminds us that it should be looked upon as another critical phase in evolutionary, and particularly human, development, comparable to the age of classical Greek culture or to the rise

---

[5] For example, Rudolf Allers, "Technology and the Human Person," *Technology and Christian Culture*, ed. Robert Paul Mohan (Washington, D.C.: The Catholic University of America Press, 1960), pp. 44–45; Dietrich von Hildebrand, "Technology and Its Dangers," *Ibid.*, pp. 72, 86.

[6] Walter J. Ong, S.J., "Christians Confront Technology, III," *America*, CI (1959), 765. In similar fashion George Sarton shows how the development of science is a continuous and cumulative growth in human experience. See *The History of Science and the New Humanism* (New York: George Braziller, Inc., 1956), chap. I, "The History of Science and the History of Civilization."

of modern science after the middle ages. In the past, the human mind has experienced sudden forward bursts in the development of culture and civilization. In fact, these bursts have been the product of man himself, prepared for by his past and assisted by the fortuitous concurrence of external conditions.

This brings us to the basic reason why the onward march of technology is inevitable. It is not the result of any necessary historical process.[7] Rather it is brought into being by the insatiable thirst of the human mind for knowledge regarding the mysteries of nature, by its restless probing as it pushes out literally into limitless space. The nature and object of that probing have differed with each age but there is no reason to suppose that the field of science and technology is any less native to the human mind than the objects to which it has devoted itself in the past.

Why, then, must we fear that this development is basically alien to man and destructive of his personality? It proceeds from an inner drive to probe the mysteries of nature. Are we to suppose that at the very moment when man has actively gained mastery over nature the latter will rise up to destroy him? In other words, are we to look upon human evolution as bearing within itself the seeds of its own destruction? Again, is the solution found in the attempt to limit evolution? [8] This would be to try to contain the human mind at some ideal point. But such a proposal is unrealistic. It is like attempting to limit the development of intelligence itself. If this attempt is made, then intelligence, like any living and growing thing, will die, for it can no longer put forth new fruits.

But one must not forget the evils attendant upon technology. Hardly anyone would deny that they are many, the most serious of which is the depersonalization of man. As a preliminary response, one might ask if these evils are really the result of technology itself. Perhaps the fault lies rather in the way in which man has approached the machine. Marston Morse adopts this view and finds a solution in the hope that men who are competent in science and who are not beguiled by mechanization will enter the fields of science and technology, will

---

[7] Dietrich von Hildebrand warns us against this exaggeration; *loc. cit.,* p. 73.

[8] This has been suggested, for example, by Frederick D. Wilhelmsen without sufficient distinctions in "Technology: Limited or Unlimited? I," *America,* XCVI (1956), 68.

handle them with respect as a body of truth to be developed, and who will make careful use of their discoveries.[9] In this way they will recover the true meaning of civilization and direct it properly in the future. On this basis, he indeed calls for a limitation of technology but one which is voluntarily adopted from a basis of understanding and not one which is forced from the outside. And he seems to wish that this limitation arise not so much from restrictions in its development as from the intelligent direction and use of that development.

Turning now to Dewey's position regarding technology, we may say that his openness to it is but an application of his fundamental principle that death follows when man does not keep pace with the ongoing process of nature, when he does not continue to develop its potentialities, his own and those of the universe in which he lives. If technology is inevitable in the sense that it is a manifestation of the onward drive of human intelligence, then man cannot but keep pace with it. If he fails to do so, it will mean the death of the human personality.

It is important that one understand clearly what Dewey is attempting to do in his approach to our modern technological age. It is not correct to say that the issue is drawn between classical culture and a technological culture in the sense that he would be trying to reduce all notions of culture to that of a machine or assembly-line. A reading of his masterful work *Art as Experience* would eliminate that idea. More than most people, he has a deep appreciation of art, literature, music, painting, sculpture, and he has no intention of doing away with these. Rather he is attempting to broaden the notion of culture so that it may not be the prerogative of the few. He lashes out against the traditional notions of culture because in his mind past ages have erected a "spiritually ornamented façade" built on the toiling masses with the result that the ordinary person, especially the worker, is spiritually impoverished.[10] At the same time, he recognizes the evils consequent upon technology. In the hope of alleviating such conditions, Dewey attempted to pinpoint their cause and to present his solution.

---

[9] Marston Morse, "Technology: Limited or Unlimited? II," *America*, XCVI (1956), 70.

[10] *Individualism Old and New* (New York: G. P. Putnam's Sons, 1930), p. 126.

The "Lost Individual"

Dewey saw that in our contemporary society man was dominated by interest in private pecuniary gain.[11] His drive for security is so influenced by our economic system that security becomes synonymous with obtaining the means of subsistence.[12] So imperious is this demand that man's higher life in terms of all that has been said regarding human fulfillment becomes blotted out. And here Dewey is not limiting this condition to times when money and the material things of life are scarce. "Even now when there is a vision of an age of abundance and when the vision is supported by hard fact, it is material security as an end that appeals to most rather than the way of living which this security makes possible." [13]

It is the enrichment of man's life that is lacking in such a situation. The most poignant manifestation of this is the fact that man today is a "lost individual." For "the significant thing is that the loyalties which once held individuals, which gave them support, direction, and unity of outlook on life, have well-nigh disappeared. In consequence, individuals are confused and bewildered." [14] Man's individuality has been submerged because he no longer has participation of imagination, intellect or emotions in the activities in which he physically participates.

> . . . economic associations are fixed in ways which exclude most of the workers in them from taking part in their management. The subordination of the enterprises to pecuniary profit reacts to make the workers 'hands' only. Their hearts and brains are not engaged. They execute plans which they do not form, and of whose meaning and intent they are ignorant—beyond the fact that these plans make a profit for others and secure a wage for themselves. To set forth the consequences of this fact upon the experience and the minds of un-counted multitudes would again require volumes. But there is an un-deniable limitation of opportunities; and minds are warped, frustrated, unnourished by their activities—the ultimate source of all constant nurture of the spirit. The philosopher's idea of a complete separation

---

11 *Individualism Old and New*, pp. 18, 31; *Liberalism and Social Action* (New York: G. P. Putnam's Sons, 1935), p. 75.

12 *Liberalism and Social Action*, pp. 59, 89.

13 *Ibid.*, p. 59.

14 *Individualism Old and New*, p. 52.

of mind and body is realized in thousands of industrial workers, and the result is a depressed body and an empty and distorted mind.[15]

On so many levels American life tends to corporateness—from the huge business mergers resulting in large corporations to social relations in leisure and recreation. Modern travel and communication are of considerable importance in this movement, for they have caused the world to shrink in time and space. This rise of social consciousness has been particularly pressing in the masses since they have arrived at a keen sense of solidarity, literally brought to a boiling point by a shared condition of misery. But on the level which most deeply concerns man and which consumes so much of his time and energy, men do not feel as members of a social whole. There is a profound maladjustment between the individual and social conditions. The individual is outwardly corporate but internally submerged. Corporateness has been achieved only externally; it must become internal, qualitative, that is, realized in thought and purpose. This abnormality gives rise to much of the unrest, irritation and hurry so characteristic of American life.

But this characteristic is not peculiar to those of the working class who are in the lower income brackets. The "captains of industry" suffer from the same malady. As justification for this position, Dewey states that "assured and integrated individuality is the product of definite social relationships and publicly acknowledged functions." [16] By this standard, even those in control of industry are submerged. For their preoccupation with private gain closes them to the deeper satisfaction that comes from the devotion of activity and energy to the good of the social whole.

> They may be captains of finance and industry, but until there is some consensus of belief as to the meaning of finance and industry in civilization as a whole, they cannot be captains of their own souls— their beliefs and aims. They exercise leadership surreptitiously and, as it were, absent-mindedly. They lead, but it is under cover of impersonal and socially undirected economic forces. Their reward is found not in what they do, in their social office and function, but in a deflection of social consequences to private gain . . . The explanation is found in the fact that while the actions promote corporate and collective results, these results are outside their intent and irrelevant to that reward of satisfaction which comes from a sense of social fulfillment.

---

[15] *Ibid.*, pp. 131–132.
[16] *Ibid.*, p. 53.

To themselves and to others, their business is private and its outcome is private profit. No complete satisfaction is possible where such a split exists.[17]

As an objection to Dewey's position, one might point to the increase of culture in American life. Regarding the *fact*, Dewey is willing to agree.

Interest in art, science and philosophy is not on the wane; the contrary is the case. There may have been individuals superior in the past; but I do not know of any time in our history when so many persons were actively concerned, both as producers and as appreciators, with these culminating aspects of civilization. There is a more lively and more widespread interest in ideas, in critical discussion, in all that forms an intellectual life, than ever before. Anyone who can look back over a span of thirty or forty years must be conscious of the difference that a generation has produced. And the movement is going forward, not backward.[18]

But Dewey will not agree as to the *interpretation* of the fact. For culture has a wider meaning. It is not restricted to the enjoyment of objects or activities which are usually accepted as artistic, esthetic or cultural. It refers also to the enrichment and meaningfulness of life on all levels. Nor is it restricted to mere numbers. It must be characteristic of a people and epoch as a whole, not merely of an elite. It is quite possible for a civilization to develop this way, that is, to build a high state of culture in certain classes of the population while the rest are submerged. "Without raising the ambiguous question of aristocracy, one can say without fear of denial that a high degree of personal cultivation at the top of society can coexist with a low and unworthy state of culture as a pervasive manifestion of social life." [19] Dewey rejects the return to this type of culture, one which consists of a spiritually ornamented façade erected on a massive substratum of material, resulting in the "spiritual disenfranciement of those permanently condemned to toil mechanically at the machine." [20] To him, there is something deeply defective in a culture which develops this way and this is not the type of culture which he envisions for America.

And yet, Dewey knows full well the pessimism of so many regarding the possibility of a culture in his sense arising from a civilization which

---

[17] *Ibid.*, pp. 53–54.
[18] *Ibid.*, p. 121.
[19] *Ibid.*, p. 122.
[20] *Ibid.*, p. 126.

is largely technological. Despite his confidence in such a civilization, he is also aware of its dangers. Hence the question is so often raised "as to whether the material and mechanistic forces of the machine age are to crush the higher life." [21] Or putting it in another way: "Can a material, industrial civilization be converted into a distinctive agency for liberating the minds and refining the emotions of all who take part in it?" [22]

Dewey is convinced that the question regarding the relation of mechanistic and industrial civilization to culture is of stupendous importance for America and one that presses for an answer. In fact, it goes much beyond the confines of our own country. It is a "problem of the world." In the minds of many Europeans, America with its technology and materialism is a threat to traditional European culture. Yet they fail to realize that the very problem which America faces is fast becoming one that the whole world will have to face. More and more countries are becoming increasingly mechanized and industrialized. Technology is on the way to becoming general. And though in this regard America has taken the lead, other countries are advancing rapidly.

Technology brings with it the problem of the despiritualization of the human personality, and Dewey is willing to admit that America has had its share of this defect. But he also knows that this danger is being faced, or will soon be faced, by European countries as well. He then raises the question as to their preparedness to face this danger. He also asks whether the weaknesses exhibited in American culture are not the result of the weaknesses of the culture she inherited.

> Transitions are out of something as well as into something; they reveal a past as well as project a future. There must have been something profoundly awry in the quality, spirituality, and individualized variety of the past, or they would not have succumbed as readily as we are told they are doing to the quantification, mechanization and standardization of the present. And the defective and perverse elements have certainly not been displaced. They survive in the present. Present conditions give these factors an opportunity to disclose themselves. They are not kept under and out of sight. Their overt manifestation is not a cheering spectacle. But as long as they did not show themselves on a scale large enough to attract notice, they could not be dealt with. I wonder very much whether many of the things that are objected to in the present scene—and justly so—are not in fact revelations of what

---

[21] *Ibid.*, p. 123.
[22] *Ibid.*, p. 124.

the older type of culture covered up, and whether their perceptible presence is not to be credited rather than debited to the forces that are now active.[23]

The elements of traditional European culture which Dewey singles out for criticism are two. The first is the early nineteenth century notion of individualism which led to the minimizing of the social aspect of man and by its *laissez-faire* economics to the submerging of the individual. The other is the exalting of the spiritual to the depreciation of the physical. This dualism alienates man from nature and prevents him from using it as a means of enriching his life.[24] The first of these two problems will be taken up in the course of the present chapter, while the second will be discussed in the last two chapters.

Dewey's answer to the question regarding the relation of our mechanistic and industrial civilization to culture is one that is favorable to the former. To him, preoccupation with commerce and wealth, and consequently with science and technology which are necessarily involved in our present civilization, is not by its very nature destructive of the higher life. The question is rather to outline the policies according to which our industrial and technological civilization may give birth to a new age of cultural enrichment for all.

The Need of "Social Awareness"

The first important step toward this goal concerns man's attitude. At present, the dominant concern of the modern American is private pecuniary gain. The important word here is "private." For Dewey

---

[23] *Ibid.*, pp. 26–27.

[24] Regarding this point, Dewey states: "A 'humanism' that separates man from nature will envisage a radically different solution of the industrial and economic perplexities of the age than the humanism entertained by those who find no uncrossable gulf or fixed gap. The former will inevitably look backward for direction, it will strive for a cultivated elite supported on the backs of toiling masses. The latter will have to face the question of whether work itself can become an instrument of culture and of how the masses can share freely in a life enriched in imagination and esthetic enjoyment. This task is set not because of sentimental 'humanitarianism,' but as the necessary conclusion of the intellectual conviction that while man belongs in nature and mind is connected with matter, humanity and its collective intelligence are the means by which nature is guided to new possibilities. Many European critics openly judge American life from the standpoint of a dualism of the spiritual and material, and deplore the primacy of the physical as fatal to any culture. They fail to see the depth and range of our problem, which is that of making the material an active instrument in the creation of the life of ideas and art." *Ibid.*, pp. 125–126.

holds no contempt for this world's goods, nor for the attempts made
by men to procure them. In fact, he maintains that it is the task of
education to train the individual to make his way in the world.[25] More
than that, the presence of material security is a favorable precondition
for the higher life.[26] On the other hand, he is also aware that a super-
abundance of material goods can be a threat to man's concern for a
higher type of life. But these points do not constitute the main problem. The thing that is most destructive of man's development and fulfillment is concern for *private* pecuniary gain which means that man
is cut off from those social relationships without which a deeper satisfaction and enrichment are impossible. And as we have already seen,
he holds that this result affects both workers and the captains of industry.

The antidote for this is the attitude of "social awareness" which on
the broader plane includes a solidarity of all men based on a profound
respect for the dignity of the human person. In Dewey's framework,
the individual is a person with capacities and potentialities that far surpass those of other natural beings in the universe, in whose hands is
committed the awesome responsibility of furthering in a corporate way
the ongoing processes of the universe and especially of men. With unity
of mind and intention men should cooperate in striving for consequences that are common to all. Hence he calls for organized planning
for chosen ends,[27] an organized integration of desires, purposes and
satisfactions of individuals, and equality through personal participation
in a *shared* culture.[28]

---

[25] "Persons cannot live without means of subsistence; the ways in which these
means are employed and consumed have a profound influence upon all the
relationships of persons to one another. If an individual is not able to earn his
own living and that of the children dependent upon him, he is a drag or parasite
upon the activities of others. He misses for himself one of the most educative
experiences of life. If he is not trained in the right use of the products of industry, there is grave danger that he may deprave himself and injure others in
his possession of wealth. No scheme of education can afford to neglect such
basic considerations. Yet in the name of higher and more spiritual ideals, the
arrangements for higher education have often not only neglected them, but
looked at them with scorn as beneath the level of educative concern. With the
change from an oligarchical to a democratic society, it is natural that the significance of an education which should have as a result ability to make one's
way economically in the world, and to manage economic resources usefully instead of for mere display and luxury, should receive emphasis." *Democracy and
Education* (New York: The Macmillan Company, 1916), p. 139.

[26] *Liberalism and Social Action*, p. 57.

[27] *Individualism Old and New*, p. 95.

[28] *Ibid.*, p. 34.

It is this sharing of values and of activities leading to these values that constitutes the community in the pregnant sense. In fact, without values prized in common, "any so-called social group, class, people, nation, tends to fall apart into molecules having but mechanically enforced connections with one another.[29] On the other hand, a community is found "wherever there is conjoint activity whose consequences are appreciated as good by all singular persons who take part in it, and where the realization of the good is such as to effect an energetic desire and effort to sustain it in being just because it is a good shared by all." [30] When all this is applied to the problem at hand, it means that Americans must break through their individual isolations and become aware of the social implications of their economic life.

Dewey could not long discuss the social and cultural aspects of man's life without becoming involved in the question of politics. For the whole question is political—and economic, too—before it is cultural.[31] Again he takes his starting point from the concern of contemporary Americans with private pecuniary gain. It is this which constitutes the main threat to man's development. But this concern is based on our present economic system of *laissez-faire* resulting from nineteenth century-individualism and liberalism. It is these latter which are the root causes of our present difficulties.

In his criticism, Dewey recognized full well the gains that had been made by earlier liberalism. "If we strip its creed from adventitious elements, there are, however, enduring values for which earlier liberalism stood." [32] These are liberty, the consequent development of individual capacities, and the central role of free intelligence in inquiry, discussion and expression. But to be grateful for a boon is not to blind oneself to "adventitious elements" which destroy much good and occasion a good deal of evil. When individualism and liberalism become connected

---

[29] *Freedom and Culture* (New York: G. P. Putnam's Sons, 1939), p. 12.

[30] *The Public and Its Problems* (New York: Holt, Rinehart & Winston, Inc., 1927), p. 149.

[31] *Individualism Old and New*, p. 124. Dewey's social and political theory would constitute a whole study in itself. We can deal with it only insofar as it affects our present problem. Dewey's treatment can be found mainly in the following works: *The Public and Its Problems, Individualism Old and New, Liberalism and Social Action,* and *Freedom and Culture.* Sidney Hook has called *Liberalism and Social Action* "a masterly analysis of the social and political philosophy of liberalism," and "a book which may very well be to the twentieth century what Marx and Engels' *Communist Manifesto* was to the nineteenth." *John Dewey: An Intellectual Portrait* (New York: The John Day Company, 1939), p. 158.

[32] *Liberalism and Social Action*, p. 32.

almost exclusively with freedom in the economic sphere and with the protection of man from any outside interference in conducting commere and industry, they give rise to *laissez-faire* resulting in the crushing of the individual. Earlier liberalism lacked an historic sense and for a while this defect was to its advantage.

> But disregard of history took its revenge. It blinded the eyes of liberals to the fact that their own special interpretations of liberty, individuality and intelligence were themselves historically conditioned, and were relevant only to their own time. They put forward their ideas as immutable truths good at all times and places; they had no idea of historic relativity, either in general or in its application to themselves.[33]

Its most glaring defect was its failure to recognize "that effective liberty is a function of the social conditions existing at any time."[34] Because of this, liberalism led to the acquiring of liberty for the few and the consequent submerging of the masses. Many proponents of earlier liberalism have tried to justify this resulting inequality by maintaining that inequality of fortune and economic status is the natural and justifiable consequence of the free play of natural inequalities in psychological and moral makeup.[35] Others glorify the individual virtues of initiative, independence, choice and responsibility.[36] Still others attribute our increase in material advantages to the existing economic system rather than to the advances made in science and technology and hence they wish to protect the *status quo*.[37] The fundamental problem remains largely untouched and the "lost individual" continues to be the victim.

Dewey did not consider that government control was the funda-

---

[33] *Ibid.,* p. 32.

[34] *Ibid.,* pp. 34–35. Again: "If the early liberals had put forth their special interpretation of liberty as something subject to historic relativity they would not have frozen it into a doctrine to be applied at all times under all social circumstances. Specifically, they would have recognized that effective liberty is a function of the social conditions existing at any time. If they had done this, they would have known that as economic relations became dominantly controlling forces in setting the pattern of human relations, the necessity of liberty for individuals which they proclaimed will require social control of economic forces in the interest of the great mass of individuals. Because the liberals failed to make a distinction between purely formal or legal liberty and effective liberty of thought and action, the history of the last one hundred years is the history of non-fulfillment of their predictions."

[35] *Ibid.,* p. 37.

[36] *Ibid.,* p. 38.

[37] *Freedom and Culture,* p. 169.

mental need. Primary in his mind was the sense of social awareness and responsibility which would lift the minds of Americans from interest in private gain and which would enlarge their vision so that they might become aware of the social whole. With this as a background, a liberal program may be developed outside of direct governmental control and may then find its way into direct political action.[38]

In this regard, Dewey believes that voluntary agreement involving captains of industry and finance on the one hand and representatives of labor and public officials on the other is more in accord with the spirit of American life than governmental coercion.[39] Without this, there will result all the evils attendant upon the enforced economic system of Soviet Russia.

Concretely, Dewey calls for the socialization of the forces of production.[40] He recognizes the gains made by "social legislation" in recent times. But these are improvisations rather than a general social policy.

> The various expressions of public control to which reference has been made have taken place sporadically and in response to the pressure of distressed groups so large that their voting power demanded attention. They have been improvised to meet special occasions. They have not been adopted as parts of any general social policy. Consequently their import has not been considered; they have been treated as episodic exceptions. We live politically from hand to mouth. Corporate forces are strong enough to secure attention and action now and then, when some emergency forces them upon us, but acknowledgment of them does not inspire consecutive policy.[41]

Liberalism must become radical, that is to say, it must result in "thoroughgoing changes in the set-up of institutions and corresponding activity to bring the changes to pass."[42] Hence his position that the forces of industry must be socialized so that the liberty of individuals may receive support and guarantee from the very structure of our

---

[38] "A liberal program has to be developed, and in a good deal of particularity, outside of the immediate realm of governmental action and enforced upon public attention, before direct political action of a thoroughgoing liberal sort will follow. This is the one lesson we have to learn from early nineteenth-century liberalism. Without a background of informed political intelligence, direct action in behalf of professed liberal ends may end in development of political irresponsibility." *Liberalism and Social Action*, pp. 15–16.

[39] *Individualism Old and New*, p. 118.

[40] *Liberalism and Social Action*, p. 88; *Individualism Old and New*, pp. 117–120.

[41] *Individualism Old and New*, pp. 114–115.

[42] *Liberalism and Social Action*, p. 62.

economic system.[43] This form of socialization Dewey calls "public" as opposed to "capitalistic," for it arises from a socially planned and ordered development rather than from the blind, determined forces issuing from an economy based on private pecuniary gain.[44] Moreover, since this form of socialism includes as a necessary condition the attitude of social awareness and responsibility, it is in no sense an extension of earlier individualism to many—a kind of fractionalized individualism.[45] It goes much deeper and extends to basic attitudes and dispositions.[46]

What, concretely, does Dewey hope will result from a system of cooperative control of industry? Regarding the workers, he has this to say:

> There would be an enormous liberation of mind, and the mind thus set free would have constant direction and nourishment. Desire for related knowledge, physical and social, would be created and rewarded; initiative and responsibility would be demanded and achieved. One may not, perhaps, be entitled to predict that an efflorescence of a distinctive social culture would immediately result. But one can say without hesitation that we shall attain only the personal cultivation of a class, and not a characteristic American culture, unless this condition is fulfilled.[47]

Elsewhere he says that the social organization envisioned by a renascent liberalism will give the opportunity for personal growth in mind and spirit for all. More immediately it will secure those material advantages which are the prerequisite for the goals envisioned, namely, a share in our cultural resources and the cooperation with others in attaining the further enrichment of these resources.[48]

---

[43] *Ibid.*, p. 88.

[44] *Individualism Old and New*, pp. 119–120.

[45] *Ibid.*, p. 81.

[46] For a fuller discussion of the type of socialism which Dewey advocated, see the books listed above, *Supra*, p. 59, footnote 31. Dewey never attempted to work out the plan in full. For his own statements in this regard, see *Liberalism and Social Action*, p. 91; *Freedom and Culture*, p. 56; "Experience, Knowledge and Value: A Rejoinder," *The Philosophy of John Dewey*, ed. Paul Arthur Schilpp, p. 592, footnote 57. For a discussion by others of Dewey's socialism as also the relation of his thought to Marxism, see Hook, *op. cit.*, chap. VIII; George R. Geiger, *John Dewey in Perspective* (New York: Oxford University Press, 1958), chap. VIII; Jim Cork, "John Dewey and Karl Marx," *John Dewey: Philosopher of Science and Freedom*, ed. Sidney Hook (New York: The Dial Press, 1950), pp. 331–350.

[47] *Ibid.*, pp. 132–133.

[48] *Liberalism and Social Action*, p. 57.

Technology and Esthetic Experience

One important question could perhaps still be asked regarding a technological age, especially regarding machine labor. Does it provide the opportunity for esthetic experience? That one would be tempted to ask such a question would indicate, in a majority of cases, that he is viewing the matter from the position of traditional culture where esthetic experience is taken in the strict sense, that is, as associated with art, literature, music, painting, and sculpture. If one starts from this standpoint, he begins with a prejudice and perhaps never will admit that work can be esthetic.

Dewey's notion of esthetic experience is much broader and can be applied to ordinary experience as well as to that which is esthetic in the technical sense. Hence his position is much more open to a fresh approach to the problem. But one thing should be noted. When we say that Dewey's notion of esthetic experience is *broader* than the traditional one, we do not mean that it is *different,* even though the media may differ. His *Art as Experience* has made this abundantly clear. One should not suppose that he has "cheapened" the notion of esthetic experience. He has merely shown that it admits of a far wider application than is usually supposed.

What is essential to Dewey's notion of esthetic experience, as we know, is the fact that man has come to terms with his surroundings. Through activity, he has reached a consummatory stage which means a unification of individual elements within the experience and of the present experience with the past and future. And the elements that are unified include not only those of the external environment but also man's own human powers and capacities. In terms which we have been using, this means that the individual has achieved human development or self-realization.

From this viewpoint, one can say that work, even as it is done with the machine, is esthetic in the instrumental meaning of esthetic, and it is precisely here that Dewey makes his most important application of the notion of the instrumental and its relation to esthetic experience. It will be recalled that esthetic experience holds the commanding position and it is to this that Dewey assigns the term consummatory. He then works out the meaning of the term instrumental by showing the difference between a *mere* means and a medium. The former is external to the thing produced; it is not a freely chosen condition leading to a freely chosen consequence. And when a mere means is considered in relation to something which is consummatory, we see that the former is anesthetic and can even be a drain and a burden.

For Dewey, mechanical work done by so many under our present industrial system in which the worker does not participate in a truly human way is the classic example of a mere means. It is the principal reason why so many Americans in our contemporary civilization lead lives which are mechanized and anesthetized in the most depressing sense. They do not freely avail themselves of certain conditions because of perceived connection with chosen consequences. Mechanical work is something they *have* to do in order to gain their goal of making money. It is not something they *want* to do, something that captures their *interest,* into which they enter with enthusiasm, spontaneity and a sense of commitment, simply because they do not have a share in the planning of the work done. Moreover—and this is in line with what Dewey says concerning the sense of social consequences—the goal of the worker is *private* pecuniary gain, not something which redounds to the enrichment of the lives of all.

Bringing to focus the principles which have been seen so far, we could say that Dewey's ideal state for the worker would be something like this. First of all, he must belong to a community in the true sense of the word, one, namely, in which there is shared activity toward shared consequences. This brings in the concept of social awareness. Thus, even though the immediate goal of a particular work done may be money and material needs, still the over-all purpose of the work is the attainment of the enrichment of the lives of all.

Secondly, the worker must have an opportunity to bring his own human capacities to bear upon the planning of the work done. In this sense, there will be freely chosen conditions leading to freely chosen consequences. The work done will be a medium and not a means because it is taken up into the consequences produced and remains immanent in them. Under these conditions, the work helps to unify and realize the individual in accordance with his present surroundings, which today are predominantly social. It helps to develop the individual as a *social being,* as a *member of a community.*

What is there that is new in this approach to self-realization? It is the greater emphasis which is placed both on community life in the development of personality and on the unique character of that community life. It is the attempt to show that human personality can best be expanded in those belonging to a community of people who undergo a similar experience, who have common goals and who cast aside their own selfish interests in the pursuit of those goals for themselves and for others. There results a liberation from that terrible isolation which stunts the human personality simply because it is turned back on itself and feeds on self. Moreover, a technological age more than any other age in the past provides the environment in and through which social awareness may be exercised, for in it people on all levels are intellectually and physically engaged in a common enterprise of providing mankind with the goods of this life. In an industrial society, more so than in past societies, human endeavor with all its various phases focuses upon common goals and common means. One might say that work as it is done in our modern age provides the matter for a closer community life into which may be infused the form and spirit of social awareness.

In approaching human self-realization from this viewpoint, one need not fall into the error of over-idealization. Though social-mindedness does away with isolationism and the depersonalization consequent upon it, there is still the opposite danger of conformity and standardization, especially in an industrialized society. Dewey recognized the danger.[49] And he is right in maintaining that this effect is not inherent in the machine. It proceeds from interest in private pecuniary gain and from the absence of *spontaneous* sharing and communication of thought and activity. The solution is found not in upbraiding science and the machine but in bringing about a radical change in man's view of modern society.

Perhaps one of the most common charges against technology, at least as far as the worker is concerned, is that machine labor is so routine and so completely absorbs the attention of the worker that he becomes immersed in the mere material work he is doing. He loses all appreciation of the meaning and dignity of his operation. As optimistic as one may be regarding the possibilities for self-realization in modern society, it must be admitted that this is a serious objection and a difficult one to answer satisfactorily. There will be no attempt, therefore, to present a

---

[49] *Individualism Old and New*, pp. 83–100. For an excellent discussion of this danger, see Rudolf Allers, *loc. cit.*, pp. 30–36. Professor Allers shows the mutual relationship between mass production, mass consumption and mass communication with their leveling effect upon the human personality.

facile or complete solution. However, before one condemns technology, a few points should be presented for consideration.

First of all, it would be difficult to defend the possibility of personality development under extreme "sweatshop" conditions. Such conditions are barely livable let alone consummatory. Hence we shall put this question aside for the time being.[50] But even if one admits that these situations are gradually being alleviated, one cannot deny that much of the work done in factories is of the assembly-line type and does not seem open to the possibility of personal development. Hence we must press on to further considerations.

For one thing, perhaps the existence, and one might say the inevitability, of assembly-line conditions can be a stimulus for modern man to look for other avenues of self-development and fulfillment than those of the classical cultural tradition. Certainly no one would consciously wish to say that personal development of the worker should be on a par with that of one who has had the advantages of a liberal education. Yet the tendency seems to be to maintain that the development of the worker should proceed through the same media. Perhaps it should rather be through different media because of the changing conditions of society in general and of the worker in particular. Dewey would say that we must exploit the possibilities for personal development inherent in community activity. Here is an avenue of human development which is new, if not in kind, then certainly in breadth and depth.

Thus Dewey has applied his theory of means and ends, his theory of the instrumental, to our present concrete conditions. He has shown that on the larger scale inquiry, technical science and technology in general have for their purpose to direct material effects, release energies and capacities, remove economic insecurity, improve the human estate so that man might attain more effectively those consummatory experiences in which consists his self-realization. It is his hope that an appreciation of these goals as the end of human endeavor will combine with the sense of "social awareness" so that man will see the meaning of the work he is doing and not become absorbed in the work itself. The goal which he sets is a lofty and ennobling one. If each person sees the relation of his activity to the goal, then it, too, will be absorbed into the end and acquire the value, dignity and even the consummatory experi-

---

[50] See *infra*, pp. 123–124.

ence of the end itself. And what is said on the larger scale of human activity in general will apply to the activity of the worker as he labors over his machine.

Of course, the problem still remains regarding the type of work which man does with the machine. Sweat-shop conditions stand at the extreme position. After that, there is a sliding scale and no attempt will be made now to locate the exact point where machine work makes self-realization practically impossible. However, it is hoped that what is said will prevent one from too easily condemning the machine worker to a depersonalized existence by approaching our industrialized society too pessimistically and thus abandoning any hope of assisting the worker to attain a satisfying life. A word should be added about the recent developments in automation and cybernetics. These would seem to present a special danger for the human person, since they take over even many of the mental operations once done by man. However, there are those who rightly maintain that such developments will rather serve to release human energy and attention from monotonous tasks of calculation and memory so that they may be engaged in tasks more fully human.[51]

Is all this too idealistic? Perhaps. But it is not nearly as overly-optimistic as the opposite view is overly-pessimistic. At the very least, it offers the worker the hope of a satisfying life instead of condemning him to a dumb, empty existence because of lack of courage to face new problems of self-realization that are posed by an industrialized society.

All this pertains to the *instrumental* aspect of work, that is, to its capacity to lead to experiences which are consummatory in themselves. Is there any sense in which work partakes of the consummatory other than in its function of being instrumental? In other words, is work consummatory as well as instrumental? Admittedly, since work is so often of a laborious nature, it does not at first glance lend itself to being inherently consummatory. This is especially true under present conditions where the worker rarely produces the whole object from beginning to end but rather is engaged merely in producing parts of the complete ob-

---

[51] See Thomas P. Neill, "Automation and Christian Culture," *Technology and Christian Culture,* ed. Robert Paul Mohan, p. 64; François Russo, "Deuxième révolution technique," *Etudes,* CCXCII (1957), 338–354; L. Malevez, S.J., "Deux théologies catholiques de l'histoire," *Bijdragen,* X (1949), 225–240.

ject. Of course, if the worker does actually produce the whole object, the work may be inherently esthetic no matter how laborious. For example, the work of an artist, sculptor, wood-carver.

However, though Dewey gives more attention to the instrumental character of work, he is aware also that at times the work done under modern technological conditions can be of itself esthetic. "Making and using tools may be intrinsically delightful," [52] and "there is something clean in the esthetic sense about a piece of machinery that has a logical structure that fits it for its work, and the polish of steel and copper that is essential to good performance is intrinsically pleasing in perception." [53] These indeed are meager examples and would scarcely satisfy the traditionalist. However, Dewey has made a beginning in striving to see esthetic experience expressed in new forms and one can hope that others will imitate his boldness and originality.

In any case, one will have to make up his own mind as to whether Dewey by his over-all approach to esthetic experience has not more than compensated for a deficiency in one area. It is our contention that he has; that is, provided that one does not expect the worker to achieve the cultural level of a trained classicist. For one thing, he has opened up the whole question of human development through participation in a community enterprise. One cannot emphasize too much the importance of this approach. In addition to the advantages already mentioned, community sharing can increase the enjoyment of works of art. In other words, because man is deprived of the opportunity to share in the planning of the work that he does and so to exercise his imagination,

---

[52] *Experience and Nature,* p. 151.

[53] *Art as Experience,* p. 342. Regarding the esthetic experience connected with things produced, Dewey says: "As for the producer of utensils, the fact that so many artisans in all times and places have found and taken time to make their products esthetically pleasing seems to me a sufficient answer. I do not see how there could be better proof that prevailing social conditions, under which industry is carried on, are the factors that determine the artistic or non-artistic quality of utensils, rather than anything inherent in the nature of things. As far as one who uses the utensil is concerned, I do not see why in drinking tea from a cup he is necessarily estopped from enjoying its shape and the delicacy of its material. Not every one gulps his food and drink in the shortest possible time in obedience to some necessary psychological law. Just as there is many a mechanic under present industrial conditions who stops to admire the fruit of his labors, holding it off to admire its shape and texture and not merely to examine into its efficiency for practical purposes, and as there is many a milliner and dressmaker who is the more engaged in her work because of appreciation of its esthetic qualities, so those who are not crowded by economic pressure, or who have not given way completely to habits formed in working on a moving belt in a speeded-up industry, have a vivid consciousness in the very process of using utensils." *Ibid.,* p. 261.

initiative and creativity, his capacity for enjoying works of art is dulled. In Dewey's mind, such stultification of human activity is more responsible for diminishing artistic appreciation than the change of landscape and all the other effects attendant upon an industrial civilization. If these obstacles are removed, man will be more open to esthetic experience.[54]

Moreover, even if we conclude that an intrinsically consummatory experience cannot be attained through machine labor, Dewey's position can heighten one's over-all sensistivity to esthetic experiences hitherto looked upon as unworthy of consideration. Again, his theory is most open to, in fact is most productive of, esthetic experience of the classical type, as *Art as Experience* shows. Hence, the worker may profit by the advantages of modern technology since it is capable of providing the leisure and financial means necessary for such experience. And this on a wider scale numerically than ever before. For example, a single television performance of a Shakespearean play is seen by more viewers than the combined performances of such a play in its whole history. One may still argue that percentage-wise citizens of previous ages did better than today. Though this could be debated, the point is that modern technology has the potential for cultural opportunities far surpassing any previous age. It remains for our socially-aware citizens to make the best use of such potential.

In his discussion of industry and technology, Dewey gave more attention to the plight of those committed to routine work with a machine than to any other group. This was natural since they form so large a part of the population and since their plight is the more pressing.[55] However, he also felt that the leaders of industry were subject to essentially the same difficulties as the working man. Although they may have a part in planning the work done, their efforts and energies are determined to the same goal of private financial gain rather than to social utility. As long as this condition obtains, they will not experience the deeper satisfaction that can come only from socially shared activities and consequences. Hence " the resulting intellectual and moral development will be one-sided and warped." [56] Remove the cause by imparting to the entire community the sense of social consciousness and responsibility and the evils of such a situation will likewise be removed. Then the captains of industry will achieve the integration and fulfillment

[54] *Art as Experience*, pp. 343–344.
[55] *Individualism Old and New*, p. 134.
[56] *Ibid.*

which result from the fact that they are making their contribution to the achievement of socially shared goals.

More than that, the leaders in industry, and in politics too, play a key role in the life of the workers. For unless they give to the latter a share in planning the community enterprises, the workers are barred from becoming a part of the community and are doomed to the fate of the "lost individual." We might add that these leaders, once imbued with the sense of community, could do much to offset the evils of technology. They would be more attentive to removing those conditions which tend to depersonalize and degrade human beings. They could see to it that men are not reduced to a commodity that can be bought and sold or to a cog in a machine that is condemned to do its job in dull, monotonous routine.

By way of conclusion to this chapter, it is well to recall once more the reason for its insertion into the present work. That reason is the relation which Dewey saw existing between self-realization and the industrial, social and political framework in which man lives. He felt that there were forces in our current civilization which were destructive of that self-realization and which demanded discussion and solution. The question is more than that of securing for all a reasonable level of material advantage, although it is certainly that, too. He is interested in this mainly insofar as it affects man's fulfillment which is his principal concern. This is substantiated by the fact that in his opinion even the captains of industry, who may reasonably be supposed to have reached considerably more than mere subsistence, may be and actually are submerged and frustrated as far as higher satisfactions and consummations are concerned. Dewey sees this condition to be the result of the presence of an individualistic outlook and the failure adequately to take into consideration the social aspect of man. His answer to this is first the development of social awareness and responsibility in the minds of the members of the community, and secondly the socialization of the forces of production. In no sense would he maintain that his treatment of the question was either final or exhaustive. In fact, he would probably admit that his work was only a beginning, an outline to be filled in during the course of subsequent human experience. But with this as a starting point, America will be well on the way towards the development of a culture calculated to achieve the enrichment of the lives of all.

V SCIENCE AND SELF-REALIZATION

So far, our discussion has dealt with only one aspect of the broad field of science, that is, science as it is found in industry and which is called technology. Explicit attention must now be given to science in its other meanings, that is, on the one hand as it includes logic or reflective inquiry and on the other as it includes the physical sciences independently of technology. More space will be given to reflective inquiry since there are some aspects of it which have important implications for a fuller picture of Dewey's thought.

Reflective Inquiry

One of the most important elements in all of Dewey's writings is his position that if the living organism fails to make proper connections with the environment so that activity is enhanced, the organism will die. This is as true for man as for any other organism. Man is engaged in a process which could mean either his highest fulfillment or his most tragic disillusionment.

Dewey was convinced, rightly or wrongly, that traditional thought, as valid as it may have been for its own cultural situation, was not adequate for present conditions. He set about to re-think the whole matter in order to develop a system of thought which would help man reach self-realization. The instrument which he felt filled the need was reflective inquiry. It forms a major part of his logical theory, or his theory of inquiry. Whether one agrees or disagrees with Dewey's theory of inquiry, one must not overlook the importance that it had in his own mind. It is meant to be a general tool with the purpose of helping man attain self-realization in the world. He felt that it must be applied to every phase of human activity; to education, morals, politics, social questions, and even to art and religion. When it makes use of specialized instruments and controlled experiments and deliberately institutes problems instead of waiting for them to arise, it becomes science in the modern sense of the term.

We have already seen that the organism develops by interaction with the environment, in which operation both organism and environment are changed. The consequence of this activity is a successful integration between the two. Man, however, takes a far more active part in the process. In him, participation in the developing course of affairs becomes deliberate and intentional.[1] Man has the power to direct the process and so to determine, control and predict the consequences. He lives in an eminent way "on the front edge of an advancing wave-crest," as William James expressed it,[2] although Dewey was more concerned than James was with developing man's part in furthering this advance. It is this power which marks off man from the lower animals.[3] It opens up in an almost unlimited way the possibilities of development both of man and of nature.[4]

It is remarkable to note how Dewey's logical theory, or theory of inquiry, is all of a piece with his theory of man's fulfillment by means of interaction with his environment. For him, the purpose of Logic is the reintegration of experience.[5] In other words, Logic is the means by which man may regain step with the ongoing movement of things, may recover his equilibrium with the moving equilibrium of nature when it has been lost and in it find fulfillment.

All this becomes evident from an examination of the early chapters of his *Logic: The Theory of Inquiry*. For example, Chapter II shows

[1] "The Need for a Recovery of Philosophy," *Creative Intelligence: Essays in the Pragmatic Attitude* (New York: Holt, Rinehart & Winston, Inc., 1917), p. 21.

[2] William James, *The Meaning of Truth* (New York: Longmans, Green & Co., Inc., 1909), p. 116.

[3] *How We Think*, 2nd ed. rev. (New York: D. C. Heath & Company, 1933), p. 17.

[4] "Of human organisms it is especially true that activties carried on for satisfying needs so change the environment that new needs arise which demand still further change in the activities of the organism by which they are satisfied; and so on in a potentially endless chain." *Logic: The Theory of Inquiry* (New York: Holt, Rinehart & Winston, Inc., 1938), p. 28.

[5] *Essays in Experimental Logic* (Chicago: University of Chicago Press, 1916), pp. 135, 183.

how the logical is connected with the biological in a process of continuous development. The biological is the existential matrix of inquiry and forms its model and pattern. He gives an account of organic life and its development which is already familiar, describing it in terms of interaction between organism and environment, disorientation and reintegration with the moving equilibrium of things, mutual development of both organism and environment.[6] These phases of organic development have already been discussed. It is sufficient merely to emphasize some specific points in order to highlight the parallel between the biological and logical.

First of all, the starting point of inquiry is the fact that man in some way has lost his integration with the environment. Because of some disturbance, he moves from a settled adjustment to a situation that is unsettled and disintegrated. The elements of an ongoing experience are in tension against one another, each contending for its proper place and relationship.[7] When a human judgment is made that the situation is indeed confused or disturbed, the situation becomes, in logical terms, problematic.[8]

Secondly, it is through logic that man achieves reintegration with the environment and a consummatory experience.[9] And in the process, there results a modification of man and environment.[10] Lastly, when the disturbed relation of organism to environment is relieved, there is not a mere return to a prior adaptive integration. Rather:

> [Inquiry] institutes new environing conditions that occasion new problems. What the organism learns during this process produces new powers that make new demands upon the environment. In short, as special problems are resolved, new ones tend to emerge. There is no such thing as a final settlement, because every settlement introduces the conditions of some degree of a new unsettling. In the stage of development marked by the emergence of science, deliberate institution of problems becomes an objective of inquiry.[11]

---

[6] *Logic: The Theory of Inquiry*, pp. 25–33.

[7] *Essays in Experimental Logic*, pp. 122–123.

[8] The technical language used by Dewey in his logical works frequently makes it difficult for the student to see the relation between his theory of inquiry and the general problem of man's integration with his environment. A constant effort is required, therefore, to keep this relationship in mind. Otherwise, the full significance of these works is lost.

[9] *Logic: The Theory of Inquiry*, p. 35. See *Essays in Experimental Logic*, pp. 135, 183.

[10] *Ibid.*, pp. 34–35.

[11] *Ibid.*, p. 35.

One cannot help but notice the similarity between his account of the logical situation and of the situation of the organism in relation to its environment. It could not be otherwise, since Dewey points out that the logical situation takes its pattern from the biological. And since the subject is man, it concerns the question of his self-realization in the universe.

Since interaction includes two elements, the organism and environment, it would be well here to point out, in large part by way of review, the characteristics of each which make the furthering of the ongoing process by inquiry possible. Inquiry presupposes as a condition the ongoing character of nature.[12] Nature is a changing world, a dynamic world, a world to be made. It is not a world "tied up in a packet without loose ends, unfinished issues or new departures."[13] The individual objects in the world, too, are not isolated, fixed, static, but changing, dynamic, capable of entering into relationships with other objects in an interaction that alters both components of the interaction.

As such, the world contains within itself almost limitless possibilities of development; things can combine and recombine in new ways, giving rise to new objects of experience and these in turn become starting points for newer objects in an endless chain. Man sets out to discover the hidden "connecting links" in nature,[14] to combine objects in new ways, and thus to further the ongoing development of nature.[15] In fact, Dewey would consider reflective thinking as a process of detecting relations.

With all his accent on the changing character of the world, Dewey does not envision a universe in chaos. There are regularities and uniformities, which, while not absolutely fixed, nevertheless give the world a character of relative permanency. It is this rhythm of stability and instability that makes logical and scientific inquiry possible.[16] In view

---

[12] See *Experience and Nature* (New York: W. W. Norton & Company, Inc., 1949), chaps. II and IV; *Reconstruction in Philosophy*, 2nd ed. (Boston: The Beacon Press, 1948), chap. III.

[13] "Does Reality Possess Practical Character?", *Essays Philosophical and Theological in Honor of William James* (New York: Longmans, Green & Co., Inc., 1908), p. 56.

[14] *Experience and Nature*, pp. 137–138; *Logic: The Theory of Inquiry*, pp. 116–117.

[15] "Flux does not have to be created. But it does have to be directed." *Liberalism and Social Action* (New York: G. P. Putnam's Sons, 1935), p. 56.

[16] *Experience and Nature*, pp. 65, 160.

of these characteristics of nature, things can be directed to new ends and new fulfillments.[17]

If the ongoing character of the world is a condition for inquiry, it is so because it is also a condition for the development of man. "Our successes are dependent on the cooperation of nature." [18] But in a finished world, "the flickering candle of consciousness would go out," [19] there would be no fulfillment; sleeping and waking would be indistinguishable.[20] Inquiry becomes not mere manipulation of inanimate things in order to bring into being new physical objects. The flux of nature can be directed to ends "in accordance with the principles of life, since life itself is development," [21] and here Dewey means human life. In fact, he states that after language the greatest single discovery for man is "the recognition that natural energy can be systematically applied, through experimental observation, to the satisfaction and multiplication of concrete wants." [22] Through control of natural forces, science has furthered this discovery by removing fear and want so that man can be free to secure for himself an ample and liberal life.[23]

But human life, too, is one of the components of the interaction by which man reaches fulfillment. And since we have examined the characteristics of the universe, it would be well to look at those of man, both by way of reviewing what has already been seen and by way of bringing in some points not yet mentioned. It is important to keep in mind that the human individual, like the nature of which it is a part, is not fixed and complete but changing and incomplete. This has already been discussed and we mention it merely to recall it. Rather we would like to revert to and enlarge on a point discussed in an earlier chapter. There it was noted that there is in man a drive onward leading him to self-realization. It is this which deserves further consideration.

The pattern for Dewey's analysis is again the biological organism.[24]

---

17 *Ibid.*, p. 159.
18 *A Common Faith* (New Haven: Yale University Press, 1934), p. 25.
19 *Experience and Nature*, p. 349.
20 *Art as Experience* (New York: G. P. Putnam's Sons, 1934), p. 17.
21 *Liberalism and Social Action*, p. 56.
22 *The Influence of Darwin on Philosophy and Other Essays in Contemporary Thought* (New York: Holt, Rinehart & Winston, Inc., 1910), p. 58.
23 *Ibid.*
24 *Experience and Nature*, pp. 252–254; *Logic: The Theory of Inquiry*, p. 27.

When the balance within a given activity is disturbed, there arises a *need* which means a condition of tension, of uneasy or unstable equilibrium. To satisfy the need, the organism will exert *effort;* that is, movement modifying environing bodies in ways which in turn react upon the organism. And if the effort is successful, it will result in a restoration of equilibrium, that is, in *satisfaction.* This sequence of *need, effort* and *satisfaction* is characteristic of every organism, including man, though human needs, activities and fulfillments are not the same as those of the lower organisms.

Dewey also speaks about *desire,* and though one is never quite sure whether or not it coincides with need or effort, its place in the ongoing movement of living beings, and hence of man, is clear.

> Desire is the forward urge of living creatures. When the push and drive of life meets no obstacle, there is nothing which we call desire. There is just life-activity. But obstructions present themselves, and activity is dispersed and divided. Desire is the outcome. It is activity surging forward to break through what dams it up. The "object" which then presents itself in thought as the goal of desire is the object of the environment *which, if it were present,* would secure a reunification of activity and the restoration of its ongoing unity. The end-in-view of desire is that object which were it present would link into an organized whole activities which are now partial and competing.[25]

The possession of the physical object is the means of removing obstructions to the ongoing, unified system of activities. It should be added that, in spite of all efforts to the contrary, discussion of human activity in terms of need and desire can lead one to suppose that in Dewey's mind man is subject to blind impulse like any biological or animal organism. But he held that pure desire, left to itself, cannot be trusted to lead to the fulfillment proper to man. Desire requires the guidance of intelligence.[26]

In the previous quotation, Dewey spoke about an object which presents itself in thought as the goal of the desire and which, if it were present, would secure a reunification of activity and the restoration of

---

[25] *Human Nature and Conduct* (New York: Holt, Rinehart & Winston, Inc., 1922), pp. 249–250.

[26] *Ibid., pp.* 254–255, 257; *Ethics,* 2nd ed. rev. (New York: Holt, Rinehart & Winston, Inc., 1932), pp. 200–201. Hence, we could conceive Dewey as re-defining desire to mean "the forward urge of living creatures under the guidance of intelligence." It must be remembered, too, that since intelligence is a characteristic of man, and man is a part of nature, then intelligence too is part of the ongoing process of nature itself.

its ongoing unity. We may now ask about the origin of that object. It is not an actually existing object, but one presented as an ideal and one to be attained. This brings us to the question of *imagination*.

Dewey calls imagination a *quality*,[27] intimately connected with the harmonizing of the self.[28] In this respect, its task is to assist man in re-integrating himself with the ongoing movement of events by proposing objects which, if present, will restore equilibrium. Imagination is singularly equipped to accomplish this, for it is *vision*,[29] which is able to see and feel things as they compose an integral whole.[30] In other words, it can project the ideal state of affairs in which man once more has a sense of unity and wholeness existing between himself and the various elements that make up his environment.

For the attainment of wholeness, there is usually necessary an object, the object of desire. It is imagination that can conjure up the object so that it may be made the goal of conscious, intelligent striving. In some cases, the object may be a familiar one, perhaps already existing and previously experienced. But imagination becomes vision in the fullest sense when it projects new objects, "through seeing, in terms of possibilities, that is, of imagination, old things in new relations serving a new end which the new end aids in creating." [31] It is concerned with the novel and adventuresome.

> When old and familiar things are made new in experience, there is imagination. When the new is created, the far and strange become the most natural inevitable things in the world. There is always some measure of adventure in the meeting of mind and universe, and this adventure is, in its measure, imagination.[32]

However, as much as Dewey insists on imagination as vision, as the ability to go beyond the present conditions of the world, he still maintains that imagination never loses its contact with the world. The aims and ideals generated through imagination "are not made out of imaginary stuff. They are made out of the hard stuff of the world of physical and social experience." [33] And though the striving of man for objects of

---

[27] *Art as Experience*, p. 267.

[28] *A Common Faith*, p. 18.

[29] *Art as Experience*, p. 268.

[30] *Ibid.*, p. 267.

[31] *A Common Faith*, p. 49.

[32] *Art as Experience*, p. 267. The relation of imagination to art is, I think, evident.

[33] *A Common Faith*, p. 49.

imagination may be the culmination of natural processes, "it is something man has learned from the world in which he occurs, not something which he arbitrarily injects into that world." [34] Again we see Dewey's reluctance to separate man's fulfillment from the world and its processes lest man lose integration with the world.

Let us return to the need-effort-satisfaction sequence in the organism and concentrate on the second phase, namely, effort. Every organism exerts some movement in order to restore its integration with surrounding conditions. As we have seen, man is unique in that he can direct and control the course of events. Reflection, or thought, assumes an intermediate and reconstructive position.

> It comes between a temporally prior situation (an organized interaction of factors) of active and appreciative experience, wherein some of the factors have become discordant and incompatible, and a later situation, which has been constituted out of the first situation by means of acting on the findings of reflective inquiry. This final situation therefore has a richness of meaning, as well as a controlled character lacking to its original. [35]

This brings us to a discussion of a very important aspect of Dewey's thought, namely, that of *idea*. It, too, has its part to play in the restoration of equilibrium. At first glance, it may seem difficult to distinguish it from imagination. Both are concerned with attaining that which is necessary in order that man may be reintegrated with his environment. But it would seem correct to say that imagination has reference more to *objects*, while idea has reference to *actions*.

Thus, when man finds himself in a situation which is disruptive of his satisfactory integration with his surroundings, or, to use logical terms, in a situation that is problematic, he studies the details of the problem. From his examination, he decides upon a course of action which is necessary in order to remove the state of disequilibrium. Consequently Dewey calls the idea a plan or method of action,[36] a guide of action;[37] it is only a tentative proposal, and hence the idea is also called a forecast, an anticipation marking a possibility,[38] a hypothesis or theory.[39]

---

34 *Experience and Nature*, p. 421.
35 *Essays in Experimental Logic*, pp. 18–19.
36 *Ibid.*, pp. 237, 240–241.
37 *Ibid.*, p. 240.
38 *Logic: The Theory of Inquiry*, p. 109; *Reconstruction in Philosophy*, p. 143.
39 *How We Think*, pp. 132–133; *Essays in Experimental Logic*, p. 312.

The validity of the idea, its effectiveness in accomplishing its purpose, must depend on test *through action*. That is, the idea, the plan, is put into operation in order to see if it will accomplish its purpose, which is the restoration of unity between man and his environment. If the plan of actions succeeds, it is true; if it fails, it is false and must be discarded for a new idea.

> Overt action is demanded if the worth or validity of the reflective considerations is to be determined. Otherwise, we have, at most, only a hypothesis that the conditions of the difficulty are such and such, and that the way to go at them so as to get over or through them is thus and so. This way must be tried in action; it must be applied, physically, in the situation. By finding out what then happens, we test our intellectual findings—our logical terms or projected metes and bounds. If the required reorganization is effected, they are confirmed, and reflection on that topic ceases; if not, there is frustration, and inquiry continues.[40]

This approach gives a whole new orientation to intelligence, thinking, reflective inquiry.[41] These are now considered in terms of *acting, doing, creating;* in brief, in terms of *process*. Thinking is considered as "directed activity," [42] a reshaper of nature and life for the well-being of man, while man himself is considered to be a responsible agent who by initiative, inventiveness and intelligently directed labor recreates the world,[43] thus projecting a better future.

For this reason, Dewey has little patience with a theory of knowledge which considers thought as reproductive of reality or as mirroring reality,[44] a position which he calls the "spectator theory" of knowledge. From this viewpoint, knowledge becomes the "blankest of stares." If man is within nature, and interaction is basic to nature, then thinking, even philosophic thinking, follows the same pattern,[45] and it, too, is an interaction without separate elements. "The view which isolates knowl-

---

[40] *Essays in Experimental Logic,* p. 13.

[41] *Experience and Nature,* pp. 158–159; *Knowing and the Known* (Boston: The Beacon Press, 1949), pp. 134–138; *Problems of Men* (New York: Philosophical Library, Inc., 1946), p. 164. See also Beatrice H. Zedler, "Dewey's Theory of Knowledge," *John Dewey: His Thought and Influence,* ed. John Blewett, S.J. (New York: Fordham University Press, 1960), pp. 59–84.

[42] *The Quest for Certainty* (New York: G. P. Putnam's Sons, 1929), p. 123.

[43] *Reconstruction in Philosophy,* p. 51.

[44] *The Quest for Certainty, pp.* 108–109; 137–139; *Essays in Experimental Logic,* pp. 250–280; *Experience and Nature,* pp. 344–353; *Knowing and the Known,* pp. 120–121.

[45] *Experience and Nature,* p. 434.

edge, contemplation, liking, interest, value, or whatever, from action is itself a survival of the notion that there are things which can exist and be known apart from active connection with other things." [46] Likewise, a theory of knowledge which in any way views the knower as separate from the known, as reproducing the known in some static way, tends to separate man from his environment, to put man "outside of and detached from the ongoing sweep of interacting and changing events." [47]

For the same reasons, he objected to a psychological approach to thinking and knowledge that concerns itself with so-called faculties or "states of consciousness," that is, sensations, images, ideas in the traditional sense. These, too, tended to put a separation between knower and known with all the evils that he felt were inevitable in such a position.[48]

In many aspects of his negative criticism, Dewey's position was unfortunate, for he closed his eyes to much that could have been fruitful for a full picture of man. He was not always a good historian of philosophy and, in many cases, did not adequately understand or appreciate traditional theories of knowledge. And for all his contributions to modern psychology, he seemed closed to some important elements of it. That fact cannot be remedied. But this should not prevent one from giving respectful attention to the positive aspects of his thought which can give new dimensions to traditional theories and which in fact cannot be ignored without detriment to philosophical development.

To conclude this section, we may now put down by way of corollaries some remarks concerning the broader topic of experience and nature. In general, Dewey's viewpoint puts stress on the future rather than on the past or present, as important as the latter may be for some purposes.

> The preoccupation of experience with things which are coming (are now coming, not just to come) is obvious to any one whose interest in experience is empirical. Since we live forward; since we live in a world where changes are going on whose issue means our weal or woe; since every act of ours modifies these changes and hence is fraught with promise, or charged with hostile energies—what should experience be but a future implicated in a present! . . . What is going on in the environment is the concern of the organism; not what is already "there" in accomplished and finished form. In so far as the issue of

---

[46] *Ibid.*, p. 435.
[47] *Ibid.*
[48] *Knowing and the Known,* pp. 120–121, 273–278.

what is going on may be affected by intervention of the organism, the moving event is a challenge which stretches the agent-patient to meet what is coming. Experience exhibits things in the unterminated aspect moving toward determinate conclusions. The finished and done with is of import as affecting the future, not on its own account; in short, because it is not, really, done with.[49]

From this aspect, experience is capable of changing the face of the world, or rather, of creating a new world; [50] it is a liberating power which frees from slavish adherence to the past and opens the way to novelty, development and progress.[51] Actual experience has always had this power, but now it becomes conscious and deliberate.[52]

The meaning of nature, too, takes on added dimensions, even when it is distinguished from man. For nature is defined not merely in terms of a universe which faces man, nor even in terms of interaction with man. This gives the impression that man and nature are two separate entities, as already existing. The meaning of nature can be extended not only in terms of things that *have* come into existence by reason of man's interaction with nature, but also in terms of things that will emerge by reason of that interaction. Thus:

> . . . nature signifies nothing less than the whole complex of the results of the interaction of man, with his memories and hopes, understanding and desire, with that world to which one-sided philosophy confines "nature." [53]
>
> From the standpoint of human experience . . ., any distinction which can be justly made between nature and man is a distinction between the conditions which have to be reckoned with in the formation and execution of our practical aims, and the aims themselves.[54]

Reflective Inquiry as Instrumental and Consummatory

It is now time to return to our original starting point and to relate reflective inquiry to esthetic experience and man's fulfillment. Reflective inquiry is to direct the future course of events. But for what end?

---

[49] "The Need for a Recovery of Philosophy," *loc. cit.,* pp. 12–13.
[50] *The Quest for Certainty,* p. 138.
[51] *Reconstruction in Philosophy,* p. 93.
[52] *Ibid.,* pp. 93–94.
[53] *Art as Experience,* p. 152.
[54] *Democracy and Education* (New York: The Macmillan Company, 1916), p. 333.

In Dewey's mind, the ultimate purpose of this direction is to attain man's fulfillment, that is, to achieve objects and situations which are consummatory. If left to themselves, events do at times bring with them their own consummations. But man has the power so to direct these events that consummations which before were casual and sporadic now become planned, directed and more plentiful.

This relation of science in the sense of reflective inquiry to the instrumental and consequently to consummatory experience is seen in the fact that Dewey relates science in the broad sense to art. First of all, he had stated that "art is a process of production in which natural materials are re-shaped through regulation of trains of events that occur in a less regulated way on lower levels of nature." [55] He then states that this is also the work of science and thus shows its relation to art. "Knowledge or science, as a work of art, like any other work of art, confers upon things traits and potentialities which did not *previously* belong to them." [56]

Speaking more explicitly of esthetic experience, he says that scientific inquiry is an art in both its instrumental and consummatory aspects.[57] Again, " 'science' is properly a handmaiden that conducts natural events to this happy issue," that is, of obtaining inherently and immediately enjoyable meanings, and "thought, intelligence, science is the intentional direction of natural events to meanings capable of immediate possession and enjoyment." [58]

The instrumental role of reflective inquiry and its relation to consummatory or esthetic experience is clear. It is sufficient merely to add two additional points. First, if reflective inquiry has an instrumental character, then all that has been said about the instrumental can and should be applied to inquiry. Thus if man *freely* avails himself of inquiry because of its *perceived* connection with *chosen* consequences,

---

[55] *Experience and Nature,* p. viii.

[56] *Ibid.,* p. 381.

[57] *Ibid.,* p. xvi.

[58] *Ibid.,* p. 358. In more technical language: "Speaking, then, from the standpoint of temporal order, we find reflection, or thought, occupying an intermediate and reconstructive position. It comes between a temporally prior situation (an organized interaction of factors) of active and appreciative experience, wherein some of the factors have become discordant and incompatible, and a later situation, which has been constituted out of the first situation by means of acting on the findings of reflective inquiry. This final situation therefore has a richness of meaning, as well as a controlled character lacking in its original." *Essays in Experimental Logic,* pp. 18–19.

the process of inquiry becomes continuous with the consummatory experience. In that case, it is not a *mere* means, external to the thing produced, but a *medium* which is "taken up into the consequences and remains immanent in them." [59] Inquiry then takes on dignity, importance and even satisfaction by being consciously related to man's fulfillment.

Second, we may reaffirm a point that has been made already, namely, that logic or reflective inquiry never loses its connection with reality. Even in its most technical and theoretical phases it maintains contact with man's real life situations inasmuch as it is ultimately geared toward obtaining for man in a more ordered and systematic way those experiences which are consummatory and which constitute his fulfillment.

So far in our discussion of reflective inquiry, emphasis has been given to what Dewey calls the "existential matrix of inquiry," which is biological.[60] But the picture would not be complete without including the "social matrix." By this is meant that inquiry is not to be conceived as something that is acquired by the individual alone. Neither is it carried out by the individual alone and for strictly private purposes.[61] This would be to return to the kind of individualism which Dewey has already rejected. The intelligence of any age is largely due to the accumulated experience of the past and when he conceives of reflection as the tool for achieving consummatory experience, it is a process that is carried out neither by the individual alone nor for the sake of the isolated individual. Inquiry, too, must be a *shared* experience, something which is characteristic of all members of the community, carried out by a cooperative effort in which methods and results are shared with others. It is also a method carried out for goals that are common to all.[62] From all that has been said above regarding Dewey's emphasis on social awareness and community, further emphasis on this aspect of inquiry need not be given here. Its application should be readily observable.

Dewey did not work out in precise detail the manner in which logic was to bring about man's fulfillment. The following passage, however, comes closest to explaining his position in this regard. "It may be that

---

[59] *Art as Experience*, p. 197.

[60] This phrase is the title of Chapter II of his *Logic: The Theory of Inquiry.*

[61] *Liberalism and Social Action*, p. 67.

[62] Jerome Nathanson calls science "organized intelligence, organized in its methods and organized socially." *John Dewey: The Reconstruction of the Democratic Life* (New York: Charles Scribner's Sons, 1951), p. 117.

general logic cannot become an instrument in the immediate direction of the activities of science or art or industry; but it is of value in criticizing and organizing tools of immediate research. It also has direct significance in the valuation for social or life-purposes of results achieved in particular branches. Much of the immediate business of life is badly done because we do not know the genesis and outcome of the work that occupies us. The manner and degree of appropriation of the goods achieved in various departments of social interest and vocation are partial and faulty because we are not clear as to the due rights and responsibilities of one function of experience in reference to others. The value of research for social progress; the bearing of psychology upon educational procedure; the mutual relations of fine and industrial art; the question of the extent and nature of specialization in science in comparison with the claims of applied science; the adjustment of religious aspirations to scientific statements; the justification of a refined culture for a few in face of economic insufficiency for the mass, the relation of organization to individuality—such are a few of the many social questions whose answer depends upon the possession and use of a general logic of experience as a method of inquiry and interpretation." [63]

But is inquiry also consummatory? Dewey does not often answer this question directly. Instead, he discusses the distinction between "esthetic" and "intellectual" experience. Judging from the way in which he speaks of the latter, we may legitimately conclude that what he says may be applied also to reflective inquiry, although in the context "intellectual" usually is broader than that and includes even technical science.[64]

That which is basic to both esthetic and intellectual experiences is the fact that each is *an* experience in the full sense of the word.[65] That is to say, each has a unity "constituted by a single *quality* that pervades the entire experience in spite of the variations of its constituent parts." [66] There is also seen the same rhythmic pattern of temporary loss of integration with the environment and its recovery followed by a sense of satisfaction and fulfillment. In this sense, an intellectual experience can be esthetic.[67]

---

[63] *Essays in Experimental Logic,* pp. 98–99.

[64] *Art as Experience,* p. 55.

[65] *Ibid.,* pp. 37–38, 55.

[66] *Ibid.,* p. 37.

[67] ". . . the pursuit of knowledge is often an immediately delightful event; its attained products possess esthetic qualities of proportion, order, and symmetry." *Experience and Nature,* p. 151.

Are we to conclude, then, that intellectual and esthetic experiences are identical? Not exactly. Although in each there is the same pattern of loss of integration followed by its recovery and consequent fulfillment, there is a difference in the point of emphasis in this fulfillment. In a distinctively intellectual experience, the main interest is in the conclusion. "The conclusion has value on its own account. It can be extracted as a formula or as a 'truth,' and can be used in its independent entirety as a factor and guide in other inquiries." [68] In a distinctively esthetic experience, however, no such precision can be made regarding the conclusion.

> In a work of art there is no such single self-sufficient deposit. The end, the terminus, is significant not by itself but as the integration of the parts. It has no other existence. A drama or novel is not the final sentence, even if the characters are disposed of as living happily ever after.[69]

An example would be the contrast between the conclusion of a mathematical problem and that of a play. The former can be detached from its context and used in further calculations but the final line of a play is meaningless without the events that have led up to it.

For this reason, the scientific man will be less disposed than the artist to rest in the conclusion. "He passes on to another problem using an attained solution only as a steppingstone from which to set on foot further inquiries." [70] The consummatory aspect of the experience is less emphasized and we see the instrumental coming forward and receiving stress.[71]

Dewey brings out this difference in a fine passage and likewise has some interesting things to say about scientist and artist.

> The difference between the esthetic and the intellectual is thus one of place where emphasis falls in the constant rhythm that marks the interaction of the live creature with his surroundings. The ultimate matter of both emphases in the experience is the same, as is also their general form. The odd notion that an artist does not think and a scientific inquirer does nothing else is the result of converting a difference of tempo and emphasis into a difference in kind. The thinker has his esthetic moment when his ideas cease to be mere ideas and become

---

[68] *Art as Experience*, p. 55.

[69] *Ibid.*

[70] *Ibid.*, p. 15.

[71] The whole question is one regarding the point of emphasis. We have already seen that the esthetic experience too is instrumental, that is, it does not come to a halt but moves on and becomes instrumental to further consummations.

the corporate meaning of objects. The artist has his problems and thinks as he works.[72]

There is a difference also in the materials with which the inquirer and the artist deal. The materials of the inquirer are symbols, words, mathematical signs, while those of the artist are tones, colors, images. Dewey adds that this is one reason why the strictly intellectual art will never be as popular as music.[73]

Technical Science as Instrumental and Consummatory

Turning now to technical science, we may begin with its instrumental aspect. Natural science has the power to direct natural events.[74] And the purpose of this direction is "to change . . . casual endings into fulfillments and conclusions of an ordered series, with the development of meaning therein involved."[75] It can regulate the date, place and manner of their emergence.[76]

It is only through the control of all the resources of science and technology that a new individualism can be achieved to replace the old. In this way, the possibilities immanent in the machine and in material civilization will help to free the latent creativity in individuals so that a new society may be created. The planned use of science will achieve for society as marvelous results as it has achieved for industrial and economic ends. Lastly, it will contribute to cultural consequences and to a liberating spiritualization by controlling the forces of nature so as to remove fear especially through the attainment of economic security.[77]

---

[72] *Ibid.,* pp. 15–16.

[73] *Ibid.,* p. 38.

[74] *Experience and Nature,* p. 148.

[75] *Ibid.,* p. 140.

[76] *Ibid.,* p. 136.

[77] See *Individualism Old and New* (New York: G. P. Putnam's Sons, 1930), pp. 93, 137–138, 143; *Philosophy and Civilization* (New York: G. P. Putnam's Sons, 1931), pp. 320–330; *The Influence of Darwin,* p. 58. Dewey is not precise regarding the manner in which science is to be instrumental for man's fulfillment. This is true whether science is taken in its general sense as reflective inquiry or in its specific sense as technical science. He was convinced, however, that science could achieve the goal he envisioned for it and that it had not been given a chance. See *Problems of Men,* p. 179; *Individualism Old and New,* pp. 93–94.

Dewey insists on the fact that science must never completely detach itself from the human condition and from social consequences. In this connection, he makes his famous distinction between "pure" and "applied" science and gives it a new meaning.[78] Unfortunately, in the minds of many, "pure" science has come to mean that which is detached from and oblivious of man's concrete condition. In this sense, it approaches the Aristotelian theory of pure contemplation. On the other hand, "applied" science has become synonymous with "utilitarian," especially in connection with private profit and class advantage.

Dewey rejects such meanings and in order to avoid ambiguity would do away with the terms. For him, science can never be separated from the ongoing sweep of events. Its primary function is that it be used by man in order to control and direct the advancing processes of nature, of which man is the spearhead. Only in this sense can it be called practical, if the term must be used. The application is for human use, convenience, enjoyment and improvement,[79] and "it includes all matters of direct enjoyment that occur in the course of living because of transformation wrought by fine arts, by friendship, by recreation, by civic affairs, etc." [80]

Once this is understood, Dewey does not object to, rather he is very much in favor of, what is called pure research. As long as science does not become "pure" in the sense of being concerned *exclusively* with objects that have no connection with human concerns, then the more research and theory the better. In fact, these are necessary if scientific procedure is to become perfected and yield more fruitful results. It will then make an important contribution to the liberation and enrichment of human experience.

From this point of view, science should be called pure or applied according to its remoteness from or proximity to the things of concrete human experience. Mathematics is "pure" in the fullest sense since it deals with symbols and signs rather than with the things of everyday life. It keeps its contact with human affairs inasmuch as its conclusions will re-enter man's concrete situation in order to further the ongoing processes of nature.

---

[78] *Experience and Nature,* pp. 161–165; *Knowing and the Known,* pp. 278–285; *The Public and Its Problems* (New York: Holt, Rinehart & Winston, Inc., 1927), pp. 174–176.
[79] *Ibid.,* p. 162.
[80] *Knowing and the Known,* p. 282.

Here again Dewey would invoke his concept of the instrumental. This would apply to science in all its phases, no matter how close or distant it is with regard to human affairs. In this sense, science is neither an end in itself, as it would be in the pejorative meaning of "pure," nor is it mere means, as it would be if "applied" meant "utilitarian." It is rather a *medium,* instrumental to consummatory experience and continuous with it and worthy of the same attention and loving care as the end to which it is ordained.

Regarding the consummatory aspect of technical science, we need do little more than recall what has already been said about the esthetic quality of intellectual activity. Dewey was not always as careful as we have been to distinguish between reflective inquiry and technical science, and what he says about one applies to the other. However, he does make an occasional reference to the esthetic quality of scientific work.

> To the layman the material of the scientist is usually forbidding. To the inquirer there exists a fulfilling and consummatory quality, for conclusions sum up and perfect the conditions that lead up to them. Moreover, they have at times an elegant and even austere form. It is said that Clark-Maxwell once introduced a symbol in order to make a physical equation symmetrical, and that it was only later that experimental results gave the symbol its meaning. I suppose that it is also true that if business men were the mere money-grubbers they are often supposed to be by the unsympathetic outsider, business would be much less attractive than it is. In practice, it may take on the properties of a game, and even when it is socially harmful it must have an esthetic quality to whom it captivates.[81]

And we have already alluded to texts where he talks about the intrinsic esthetic quality in the making and using of tools and in the products of industry.

In general, one may be struck by the seeming reticence exhibited by Dewey in speaking of the consummatory aspect of both reflective inquiry and technical science. He always seems afraid lest he give too much emphasis to this aspect of intellectual experience. One reason for this seems to be that such an emphasis will lead to the glorifying of intellectual experience for its own sake.[82] This would contradict his whole polemic against the Greek theory that contemplation is the high point in man's life. This theory leads (for Dewey) to the separa-

---

[81] *Art as Experience,* pp. 198–199.
[82] *Experience and Nature,* pp. 107, 118–119, 161–165.

tion of man from nature and the consequent interruption of the on-going process.

Another reason is that if science becomes separated from the human condition, then almost by default it will be won over to the cause of private pecuniary gain. Our own age has actually witnessed the disastrous results of such a condition.

> It has maintained sordid slums, flurried and discontented careers, grinding poverty and luxurious wealth, brutal exploitation of nature and man in times of peace and high explosives and noxious gases in times of war. Man, a child in understanding of himself, has placed in his hands physical tools of incalculable power. He plays with them like a child, and whether they work harm or good is largely a matter of accident. The instrumentality becomes a master and works fatally as if possessed of a will of its own—not because it has a will but because man has not.[83]

This is the result of separating science from the human condition. Man becomes incapable of understanding his own affairs and of directing them.[84]

Perhaps at times this bias does prevent him from giving fuller attention and greater amplification to the strictly consummatory aspects of inquiry and technical science. But no one can deny that he was keenly aware and appreciative of this aspect of intellectual experience. His attitude would seem to be: Never lose your awareness that the survival and development of man depends on his continued contact with the ongoing process of nature; never lose contact with that process. Keep up with it, continue it, forward it. For the rest, drink to the full the consummatory aspects of experience wherever you may find them, open yourself to them, accept them, seek them, actively foster them through inquiry and technical science. And even experience the joys of these latter. But do not make of intellectual activity the "end of ends, for the sake of which all else happens." [85]

The Task of Intellectuals

The discussion of reflective inquiry and technology leads quite naturally to another segment of the population with which Dewey was concerned. That segment includes the intellectuals and their place in

---

[83] *The Public and Its Problems,* p. 175.
[84] *Ibid.,* p. 176.
[85] *Experience and Nature,* p. 119.

contemporary society must be considered. For they, too, can and have become "lost individuals" just as workers and captains of industry.[86]

At the outset, one might ask just what is an intellectual. Merle Curti,[87] in a statement accepted by O'Dea,[88] defines intellectuals as "those men and women whose main interest is the advancement of knowledge, or the clarification of cultural issues and public problems." O'Dea goes on to say that they are those "committed to the intellectual solution of human problems," [89] including creative artists and critics. Though Dewey gives no precise definition, he would certainly have no objection to such formulations. Among intellectuals he includes "philosophers, professional and otherwise, critics, writers and professional persons in general having interests beyond their immediate callings." [90] In any case, it is not necessary to indulge in endless definitions and refinements. The meaning as stated above is sufficient for our present purposes.

Dewey acknowledges the fact that intellectuals have not been without influence in the past. But that influence has not been in proportion to their potential. The reason is that the intellectual activity of this class of citizens has been dispersed and divided, and so they too become "lost individuals." [91] The main cause has been a kind of "mental withdrawal" from the problems presented by an industrialized society. Intellectuals as a group have generally not been conscious of their responsibility which is to make such a society a servant for human life—"a problem which is once more equivalent, for us, to that of creating a genuine culture." [92]

Certainly Dewey would set down as a primary requisite for such a function the sense of "social awareness" which is so much a part of his whole view of modern civilization. Intellectuals, as much as workers and leaders of industry, must become truly members of the community.

---

86 For a discussion of this problem, see Merle Curti, *American Paradox: The Conflict of Thought and Action* (New Brunswick, N. J.: Rutgers University Press, 1956). This same problem is taken up by Thomas F. O'Dea, *American Catholic Dilemma: An Inquiry into the Intellectual Life* (New York: Sheed & Ward, 1958), pp. 21–34, although his development of this theme moves along quite different lines.

87 Curti, *op. cit.*, p. 73.

88 O'Dea, *op. cit.*, p. 22.

89 *Ibid.*

90 *Individualism Old and New*, pp. 138–139.

91 *Ibid.*, p. 139.

92 *Ibid.*, p. 141.

They must open their minds to the common goal of all members of society, which is the achievement of a truly human life for all. Likewise, they must devote their attention and energies in a cooperative effort to take the means necessary for that achievement.

The type of activity in which intellectuals will engage must be in keeping with their calling. And here Dewey wants to make sure that he is not misunderstood.

> This point of view is sometimes represented as a virtual appeal to those primarily engaged in inquiry and reflection to desert their studies, libraries, and laboratories and engage in works of social reform. That representation is a caricature. It is not the abandonment of thinking and inquiry that is asked for, but more thinking and more significant inquiry. This "more" is equivalent to a conscious direction of thought and inquiry, and direction can be had only by a realization of problems in the rank of their urgency. . . . A more intimate connection [with the scenes of action] would not signify, I repeat, a surrender of the business of thought, even speculative thought, for the sake of getting busy at some so-called practical matter. Rather would it signify a focussing of thought and intensifying of its quality by bringing it into relation with issues of stupendous meaning.[93]

Immediately evident here is the connection of this position with his views on "pure" and "practical" science. The same theme runs through all his thinking, namely, that attention of the members of the community on all levels must be directed, either immediately or mediately, toward the achievement of man's fulfillment and toward the solution of those problems which hinder that fulfillment. This approach gives the lie to those who picture Dewey as an anti-intellectual wanting nothing more than to engage American citizens in tinkering with gadgets. Primary in his mind is a sense of social calling and commitment which must be characteristic of every member of the community. The manner in which this awareness is actualized will depend on the talent, capacity and the preference of each individual.

There is a connection of all this, too, with what has been said regarding reflective inquiry or scientific method in the large sense. This is the main tool by which the intellectual is to carry out his work. It is the reflective inquiry which is developed in Dewey's more technical works, such as *Essays in Experimental Logic* and *Logic: The Theory of Inquiry*. It is a general method that can be mastered and used by ex-

---

[93] *Ibid.*, pp. 139–141.

perts, each in his own field.[94] In the following passage, Dewey reviews the main lines of this logic of method and makes the necessary application to social consequences.

> Such a logic involves the following factors: First, that those concepts, general principles, theories and dialectical developments which are indispensable to any systematic knowledge be shaped and tested as tools of inquiry. Secondly, that policies and proposals for social action be treated as working hypotheses, not as programs to be rigidly adhered to and executed. They will be experimental in the sense that they will be entertained subject to constant and well-equipped observation of the consequences they entail when acted upon, and subject to ready and flexible revision in the light of observed consequences. The social sciences, if these two stipulations are fulfilled, will then be an apparatus for conducting investigation, and for recording and interpreting (organizing) its results. The apparatus will no longer be taken to be itself knowledge, but will be seen to be intellectual means of making discoveries of phenomena having social import and understanding their meaning.[95]

It is not out of place at this point to emphasize once more how important for Dewey's whole philosophic enterprise is his logic, theory of inquiry, reflective inquiry, scientific method, or whatever else one may wish to call it. He has dealt with this topic at great length and in very technical language. But he never meant that it remain hidden within the covers of a book as a scholarly exercise. For him it was a tool, the only tool, for furthering the ongoing process of man in the never-ending achievement of fulfillment and for coming to grips with those problems that in each age threaten to stall that progress. Until this tool is mastered and universally applied to human problems, man will never reach the stage of development in accordance with his capacities.

This does not mean, however, that Dewey intended to limit the method of reflective inquiry to experts, to intellectuals. This would seem to be so if we confined our attention to his more technical handling of this method as found in his strictly logical works. The full import of these works would seem to be beyond the scope and ability of the masses and hence to be limited to a comparatively few. But when we look into his works which deal with education and thinking, notably *Democracy and Education* (especially Chapters XI, XII and XIII), and *How We Think,* it is quite clear that he is proposing a method of re-

---

94 *The Public and Its Problems,* pp. 208–209.
95 *Ibid.,* pp. 202–203.

flective inquiry which is meant for everyone. Here we see the same concept of knowing as doing and as direction; the same sequence of facing the indeterminate situation, instituting the problem, projecting and testing hypotheses and checking the consequences as is found in more technical language in the logical works. And certainly anyone familiar with Dewey's educational theory will realize that it is geared toward imparting to the student the experimental method of dealing with real-life situations.

The task, then, of directing social consequences is not the work of experts alone. All members of the community are to have at their command some knowledge of the method of inquiry, at least sufficient and necessary for them to share in the furthering of social consequences according to their capacity and position. In more complicated matters, the "many" will have to wait upon the conclusions of the experts. Then their task will be "to judge of the bearing of the knowledge supplied by others upon common concerns." [96] It is for them to take the results of scientific investigators and apply them to the concrete situation.

And in this latter function, Dewey warns us not to exaggerate the amount of intelligence and ability needed. Until now cooperative effort has not been carried out on any large scale and so we have no way of knowing how apt the masses are for making sound judgments regarding social policy. Besides, the knowledge readily available at present is quite considerable, for each age benefits by the accumulated wisdom of the past. It is astounding to think, for example, that a mechanic today knows more about electricity than a Sir Isaac Newton knew, or that a tinker in radios knows more about such matters than a Faraday was able to imagine. We should have confidence in the store of knowledge available to the "many" and look upon the direction of social consequences as an effort in which all may participate. It is a task to be done "by the resolute, patient, cooperative activities of men and women of good will, drawn from every useful calling, over an indefinitely long period." [97]

---

[96] *Ibid.*, p. 209.

[97] *Reconstruction in Philosophy*, p. xxxv. There remains the important question regarding the intellectual, and that concerns the achievement of fulfillment and self-realization. Actually, this question has already been discussed in the treatment of the instrumental and consummatory in relation to reflective inquiry and technical science. *Supra*, pp. 63–70, 81–89. What has been said there applies also to the intellectual, for the man of technical science and of technical reflective inquiry would be an intellectual in the sense explained.

Education

The ideal of community and its function of directing social consequences envisioned by Dewey could hardly be realized without a theory of education. For "we are not born members of a community. The young have to be brought within the traditions, outlook and interests which characterize a community by means of education: by unremitting instruction and by learning in connection with the phenomena of overt association." [98] Hence, it would be well to examine Dewey's theory of education, not in all its aspects, for that would require a separate study, but in those aspects that most pertain to the present discussion.

The attitude of social awareness is most essential for the community in all its implications. Here education has an important role to play in imparting to the young an appreciation of this attitude. But it is precisely here that in Dewey's opinion education in America has been most deficient. As a result, the distinguishing trait of our students on the higher levels is intellectual immaturity regarding social problems.

> This immaturity is mainly due to their mental seclusion; there is, in their schooling, little free and disinterested concern with the underlying social problems of our civilization. Other typical evidence is found in the training of engineers. Thorstein Veblen—and many others have since repeated his idea—pointed out the strategic position occupied by the engineer in our industrial and technological activity. Engineering schools give excellent technical training. Where is the school that pays systematic attention to the potential social function of the engineering profession?
>
> I refer to the schools in connection with this problem of American culture because they are the formal agencies of producing those mental attitudes, those modes of feeling and thinking, which are the essence of a distinctive culture. But they are not the ultimate formative force. Social institutions, the trend of occupations, the pattern of social arrangements, are the finally controlling influences in shaping minds. The immaturity nurtured in schools is carried over into life. If we Americans manifest, as compared with those of other countries who have had the benefits of higher schooling, a kind of infantilism, it is because our own schooling so largely evades serious consideration of the deeper issues of social life; for it is only through induction into realities that the mind can be matured.[99]

---

[98] *The Public and Its Problems*, p. 154.
[99] *Individualism Old and New*, pp. 127–129.

Dewey goes on to say that without this training in social awareness the graduate is unprepared to meet the conditions of adult society where there is an exaggerated emphasis on success in business. The student is not prepared to meet this influence and hence adopts the "business mind." He is unable to resist and so does not have "the vision and desire to direct economic forces in new channels." [100]

Democracy and Education, which first appeared in 1916 (and hence well before the developed works on the social order), shows that Dewey was already aware of the important relation between education and social questions. This relationship appears again and again, and is integral to his whole concept of education.

For example, in Chapter VII called "The Democratic Conception in Education," he discusses society in terms of shared aims and shared activity in the pursuit of such aims. He then adds:

> Such a society must have a type of education which gives individuals a personal interest in social relationships and control, and the habits of mind which secure social changes without introducing disorder.[101]

In this sense, education is a "social process" and the burden of the chapter is to show the relationship between education and society.

In Chapter IX, entitled "Natural Development and Social Efficiency as Aims," the idea is pursued further. Even before the more fully developed works on the social order, Dewey is seen criticizing nineteenth century liberalism with its isolation of the individual, and focusing attention on the importance of communal life and training for participation in such life. In speaking of social efficiency, he says that it is "nothing less than that socialization of *mind* which is actively concerned in making experiences more communicable; in breaking down the barriers of social stratification which make individuals impervious to the interests of others." [102] The two things necessary in this connection are sympathy or good will, which he would probably equate with "social awareness," and overt action, which would mean the active direction of social consequences. It is in this service to others that the members of the community will find experiences that are inherently worthwhile, whether they be farmers, physicians, teachers or students.[103]

---

[100] *Ibid.*, p. 129.
[101] *Democracy and Education*, p. 115.
[102] *Ibid.*, p. 141.
[103] *Ibid.*, p. 143.

In a section called "Subject Matter as Social," found in Chapter XIV, he discusses the relation of the school curriculum to society. Studies should be chosen according to the needs of the community so that the life which we share in common may be improved in the future.[104] Observation and information should be selected with a view to developing social insight and interest.[105]

Dewey's theory of education is alive also to the tool with which the members of the community are to direct social consequences and hence it gives ample consideration to reflective inquiry. This has already been mentioned in passing.[106] But it would be well to spend more time on it.

In the original 1910 edition of *How We Think*, Dewey wrote a Preface, repeated in the revised edition of 1933, in which he explains the purpose of the book. It was written for harassed teachers who find themselves swamped with the numerous studies that must be imparted, each with its own materials and principles, and with the task of giving students individual attention. He wanted to simplify their task by supplying a principle of unity. He therefore felt that the best results could be obtained by imparting to the students the scientific method. Hence he states:

> This book represents the conviction that the needed steadying and centralizing factor is found in adopting as the end of endeavor that attitude of mind, that habit of thought, which we call scientific. This scientific attitude of mind might, conceivably, be quite irrelevant to teaching children and youth. But this book also represents the conviction that such is not the case; that the native and unspoiled attitude of childhood, marked by ardent curiosity, fertile imagination, and love of experimental inquiry, is near, very near, to the attitude of the scientific mind. If these pages assist any to appreciate this kinship and to consider seriously how its recognition in educational practice would make for individual happiness and the reduction of social waste, the book will amply have served its purpose.[107]

That Dewey's opinion did not change in twenty-three years is shown by the fact that in the later edition he not only retained the basic ideas but enlarged upon them. And the section which received the greatest

---

104 *Ibid.*, p. 225.

105 *Ibid.*, p. 226.

106 *Supra*, pp. 94–95. For an excellent discussion of scientific inquiry in its relation to education and democracy, see Sister Joseph Mary Raby, S. S. J., "John Dewey and Progressive Education," *John Dewey: His Thought and Influence*, pp. 85–115.

107 *How We Think*, p. iii (1910 ed.); p. v (1933 ed.).

amplification is Part II on "Logical Considerations." Containing nine chapters and comprising almost half of the book's three hundred or more pages, it includes the heart of Dewey's theory on reflective thinking and the scientific method.

Democracy and Education, appearing in 1916 between the earlier and later editions of *How We Think,* likewise gives attention to reflective inquiry. It could not be expected to deal with this topic with anywhere near the thoroughness of the other work, since it ranges over a much broader field with a greater variety of topics and problems. However, in four different places it handles aspects of reflection and again sets down Dewey's basic ideas on the subject.[108]

Turning now to technical science, we find that it, too, had received Dewey's attention in its relation to education. He maintained that the manner in which science is taught is another reflection of the inchoate state of our social knowledge.

> Science is taught in our schools. But very largely it appears in schools simply as another study, to be acquired by much the same methods as are employed in "learning" the older studies that are part of the curriculum. If it were treated as what it is, the method of intelligence itself in action, then the method of science would be incarnate in every branch of study and every detail of learning. Thought would be connected with the possibility of action, and every mode of action would be reviewed to see its bearing upon the habits and ideas from which it sprang. Until science is treated educationally in this way, the introduction of what is called science into the schools signifies one more opportunity for the mechanization of the material and methods of study. When "learning" is treated not as an expansion of the understanding and judgment of meanings but as an acquisition of information, the method of cooperative experimental intelligence finds its way into the working structure of the individual only incidentally and by devious paths.[109]

Since this deficiency in the teaching of science is a reflection of the inchoate state of social knowledge, it is clear that Dewey wants the teaching of science to equip the student with the means necessary for the eventual direction of social consequences.

In *Democracy and Education,* he explains how science has been the means of bettering our common human estate. However, these effects

---

108 *Democracy and Education,* "Reflection in Experience," pp. 169–177, "Science or Rationalized Knowledge," pp. 221–226, "Experience as Experimentation," pp. 317–322, "Individual Mind as the Agent of Reorganization," pp. 343–351.
109 *Liberalism and Social Action,* pp. 46–47.

have been due to the growth of science itself rather than to deliberate planning. "The problem of an educational use of science is then to create an intelligence pregnant with belief in the possibility of the direction of human affairs by itself." [110]

Conclusion

The guiding principle of this section, as of everything said so far, is the over-all purpose of Dewey's whole philosophic enterprise. This was seen to be his concern for working out the conditions for man's self-realization in terms of consummatory experience. In Dewey's mind, a serious obstacle to that fulfillment in the thinking of many is science and technology. Dewey takes the firm stand that the technological development of our industrialized society is not of itself detrimental to or destructive of man's fulfillment. The fault lies rather in the purpose to which technology is directed. This purpose he sees to be private pecuniary gain.

Dewey offers two solutions to the problem. First, he advocates the attitude of social awareness on the part of every member of society. This means shared goals and shared activity in the attainment of those goals. If this attitude is adopted, our social and economic system will rid itself of that individualism and egoism which stifle human personality and prevent it from reaching its full development. We see here the application of a notion fundamental to Dewey's concept of experience. For him, human experience is an interaction of persons with things and with other persons. Important for this whole concept is what he has called "the social as philosophic category." Without the social element, the human person cannot expand and find its development and enrichment.

His second solution to the problem involves showing man how he can deal fruitfully with matter. On the wider scale, he has already shown how the things of everyday life can lead to an experience which is genuinely esthetic and he has thus labored to eliminate the distinction between ordinary experience and experience which is called esthetic or artistic in the technical sense. In this regard, he had worked out the theory of the instrumental and consummatory in order to bring every

---

[110] *Democracy and Education,* p. 263.

type of object and activity into the area of the esthetic and hence into the area of man's fulfillment. These principles are applied to the problem of technology. The objects and activities of our industrialized economy are not of themselves hostile to man's fulfillment. If handled correctly, they can further the ongoing process of man toward self-realization.

It is seen, then, that Dewey's treatment of science and technology is but a specific application of his over-all attempt to show man how he can reach fulfillment in and through matter. He believed that if his theory is followed and applied, man will be able to cope with nature and by this means, indeed by this means alone, reach that development of which the human person is capable. Science will then be seen in its active incarnation rather than in theoretical abstraction.[111]

Dewey felt, too, that his theory would help to develop a culture which is characteristically our own.[112] In America, specific problems have come into focus which demand specific answers: problems of technology, science, education, society, politics. In his mind, the older form of liberalism and individualism inherited from a European tradition is no longer adequate to the present circumstances. There is need of a new culture and a new philosophy peculiarly American in order to cope with present conditions.[113]

And yet, from another point of view, the problem that America faces is not peculiar to itself. It is the "problem of the world." Technology will some day become a world-wide problem, and this is perhaps even truer today than it was in the mid-thirties when Dewey was writing on these problems. America has gained much from European culture and Dewey is not blind to the debt we owe to it in spite of his sometimes harsh criticism regarding its full application today. But he now envisions the day when America will develop an "indigenous culture," the creation of which "is no disservice to the traditional European springs of our spiritual life. It will signify, not ingratitude, but the effort to repay a debt." [114]

---

111 *Ibid.*, p. 336.

112 *Individualism Old and New*, pp. 136–137.

113 *Ibid.*, *passim*; "The Need for a Recovery of Philosophy," *loc. cit.*, pp. 66–69; *Philosophy and Civilization*, pp. 3–12; *Art as Experience*, pp. 339–340.

114 *Individualism Old and New*, p. 142.

VI   THE MEANING OF DEWEY'S NATURALISM

Perhaps the charge most frequently leveled against Dewey by those who oppose his thought is that it is "naturalistic." This is a word with many meanings, as Dewey himself admitted.[1] It includes overtones that are atheistic, materialistic, anti-supernaturalistic, anti-religious. In some sense, Dewey's thought is all of these things though the precise meaning of these terms as applied to his thought should be refined further.

Perhaps it would be well to state just what Dewey's naturalism would include. Fundamentally and above all else, it is a naturalism "which perceives that man with his habits, institutions, desires, thoughts, aspirations, ideals and struggles, is within nature, an integral part of it." [2] Expressed in other terms, it means that "man's life is bound up in the processes of nature; his career, for success or defeat, depends upon the way in which nature enters it." [3] The previous chapters, it is hoped, have spelled out in detail what these sentences mean. For it was seen that at the basis of Dewey's naturalism is his insistence on man's continuity with nature and on the fact that man can achieve self-realization only in and through nature.

In adopting this position, Dewey was profoundly influenced by his study of the conditions under which organisms, including man, develop. From biology, evolution, social psychology and anthropology, he was deeply impressed with the fact that organisms develop only in and through an environment. This led him to his classic theory of "inter-

---

[1] *Individualism Old and New* (New York: G. P. Putnam's Sons, 1930), p. 153.

[2] *Ibid.*

[3] *Democracy and Education* (New York: The Macmillan Company, 1916) p. 267.

100

action." The insight grew into the dominating conviction that the living being can neither survive nor develop without its material environment and that any position which separates man from it will seriously hinder the ongoing process of nature.

From this basic position follow two corollaries. First, Dewey's outlook pretends to be totally "intra-mundane." Nothing can be admitted which transcends the possibilities of concrete, human experience. There is no Absolute, no transcendant being, no extra-mundane reality. A second corollary is the position that there is no room for a supernatural religion. In a sense, this corollary is identical with the preceding, since for Dewey "supernatural" means that which transcends the possibilities of concrete human experience and involves an Absolute Being. The latter is excluded in Dewey's framework and this is why he substitutes the word "religious" for "religion." So important is this approach for an understanding of Dewey's naturalism and of his whole theory of self-realization that it deserves to receive special consideration.

Religious Experience

Dewey scholars have not always been in exact agreement as to the proper relationship of religious experience to esthetic experience. For Irwin Edman, art is the high point of Dewey's theory of experience and of his philosophy.[4] George Geiger agrees with this and seems to see little or no difference between religious and esthetic experience.[5] Sidney Hook merely discusses each separately without any attempt to show the relationship between the two.[6] Yet there would seem to be discernible in Dewey's notion of religious experience a dimension which goes beyond esthetic experience, consisting in the unification of the self with environment on a deeper and more expansive level. It is this dimension which we shall attempt to emphasize in our treatment of religious experience.

The first thing that may be said of Dewey's approach, distinguishing

---

[4] Irwin Edman, "Dewey and Art," *John Dewey: Philosopher of Science and Freedom*, ed. Sidney Hook (New York: The Dial Press, 1950), pp. 48–49, 65.

[5] George R. Geiger, *John Dewey in Perspective* (New York: Oxford University Press, 1958), pp. 19–20, 38, 214.

[6] Sidney Hook, *John Dewey: An Intellectual Portrait* (New York: The John Day Company, 1939), chaps. X, XI.

it from other approaches, is that an experience is called "religious" not because of that from which it proceeds but rather because of that to which it leads.[7] A more traditional approach would be to call an experience religious if it is rooted in or proceeds from belief in the divine or in some tenet related to the divine. From this point of view, religious experience is something unique and clearly distinct from the experiences of daily life.

For Dewey, however, an experience is religious in as much as it effects the integration of the individual with surrounding conditions. Here we must again keep in mind his position regarding the achievement of harmony and fulfillment through integration with the environment. This involves interaction in which both the organism and the surrounding conditions are changed for the better. There are degrees of perfection in this integration according to the increasing complexity of the organism, ranging from the lowest biological organism, through animals, to man. And with man, too, there are degrees. The changes in primitive man and his surroundings are much less varied and perfect than are the changes in modern man and his surroundings.

Furthermore, since the process of nature, including man, is ongoing, there is an indefinite range of possibilities that can be activated both in man and in the universe through their interaction. As for man himself, his personality is being shaped, created and realized. And since this process is on a scale of increasing perfection, we can conceive of man as being more perfectly realized, as reaching deeper and more perfect harmony of self with the environment. Hence, since man's increasing self-realization consists in the continual activation of an infinite range of possibilities both in man and in the universe, the imagination unites into a single ideal and projects into the future all possibilities existing in man and in the universe and relates them to one another by the fact that these possibilities can be actualized through human endeavor, that is, through interaction. There is formed an idea of a whole, both of the whole personal self and of the whole world. These latter are not actually existing things; they cannot be grasped in knowledge nor can they be realized through reflection.[8] They are imaginative extensions of all the possibilities existing in the self and in the world. These ideal states are not conceived in separation, since there is also included in this ideal an

---

[7] *A Common Faith* (New Haven: Yale University Press, 1934), p. 14.

[8] *Human Nature and Conduct* (New York: Holt, Rinehart & Winston, Inc., 1922), p. 263.

active relationship between self and the universe consisting of the possible activities and operations through which man will be able to achieve his increasing development.[9] *When this imaginative unification is achieved, man is said to have a religious experience.*

From this it is seen that Dewey's theory of religious experience is but another application of his attempt to work out the conditions for self-realization. Like every other experience discussed so far, it is expressed in terms of integration with surrounding situations. And yet, it is a much wider and deeper experience than any other. For one thing, "religious" is a quality that may belong to all experiences, for example, scientific, moral, political, to experiences of companionship and friendship, and even to the esthetic.[10]

If we approach experience from the point of view of harmony and integration, we can again detect a difference between the esthetic and religious. Dewey returns to the example of adjustment to environment. There are various ways in which an organism can regain harmony with its surroundings. Thus, in particular and limited conditions, we modify our particular attitudes in accordance with the environment, for example, the weather, when no other alternative is possible. In this case, only *particular modes* of our conduct are affected, *not the entire self,* and in the process we are for the most part *passive.* This process he calls *accommodation.*

In other cases, however, we react to conditions and change them according to our wants and demands. For example, we rebuild a house to suit altered conditions; we invent a telephone to fulfill the need for speedy communication at a distance; we irrigate the soil for more abundant crops. These processes are still *particular,* that is, they do not affect the *entire self,* although they are more *active,* and are called *adaptations.*[11]

Lastly, there is the experience which is called *religious,* which means that

> . . . there are also changes in ourselves in relation to the world in which we live that are much more inclusive and deep seated. They relate not to this and that want in relation to this and that condition of our surroundings, but pertain to our being in its entirety. Because of their scope, this modification of ourselves is enduring. It lasts through

---

[9] *A Common Faith,* pp. 19, 33, 49.
[10] *Ibid.,* p. 10.
[11] *Ibid.,* pp. 15–16.

any amount of vicissitude of circumstances, internal and external. There is a composing and harmonizing of the various elements of our being such that, in spite of changes in the special conditions that surround us, these conditions are also arranged, settled, in relation to us.[12]

We may note that religious experience is conceived in terms of the harmonizing of the self in relation to surrounding conditions. But there is a hint here of something more. Experience, outside of the religious, is always described more as an integration of the *present* self with *present* environment. This is true even of esthetic experience, despite the fact that there is also included a sense of continuity with a whole. For even though this sense of wholeness has degrees of intensity and is rendered more intense and more explicit in a work of art, it is still secondary to the integration of the self at the present moment. It is this latter element that is still dominant.

But in the above text, and especially in all that we have seen so far, religious experience pushes on further still. There is a quality which goes beyond the integration of the present moment and involves the imaginative idea of the unification of the *whole* self with the *whole* universe through an ongoing process of interaction. Hence, the changes in ourselves in relation to the world are more inclusive and deep seated. They concern not this or that condition of the environment but pertain to our whole being.

Dewey develops the same theme from another starting-point. He intends to show the nature of imagination as it is found in religious experience. To bring out his point, he contrasts it with imagination of esthetic experience.[13] He uses as a basis of discussion a treatment given to imagination by Santayana.

Mr. Santayana has connected the religious quality of experience with the imaginative, as that is expressed in poetry. "Religion and poetry," he says, "are identical in essence, and differ merely in the way in which they are attached to practical affairs. Poetry is called religion when it intervenes in life, and religion, when it merely supervenes upon life, is seen to be nothing but poetry." The difference between intervening *in* and supervening *upon* is as important as is the identity set forth. Imagination may play upon life or it may enter profoundly into it. As Mr. Santayana puts it, "poetry has a universal and a moral

----

[12] *Ibid.*, p. 16.
[13] It seems clear that Dewey intends esthetic experience, since he uses the example of poetry.

function," for "its highest power lies in its relevance to the ideals and purposes of life." . . . If I may make a comment upon this penetrating insight of Mr. Santayana, I would say that the difference between imagination that only supervenes and imagination that intervenes is the difference between one that completely interpenetrates all the elements of our being and one that is interwoven with only special and partial factors.[14]

Esthetic experience involves only "special and partial factors." This means that there is achieved a temporary sense of harmony after a previously disturbed condition. For the present moment, at least, surrounding conditions are settled in a manner satisfactory to the wants and needs of the self. In saying that esthetic experience involves "only special and partial factors," Dewey does not intend to press this in too narrow a fashion. Taken literally, such a harmony between the organism and the environment would apply even to biological and animal organisms. And certainly he would not call these integrations "esthetic." He shows that he has an appreciation for the fact that on the human level, the harmony involved does not mean satisfaction of this or that need. In a truly esthetic experience, there is in some sense a fulfillment of the whole person in relation to his environment and here he seems to mean more the depth of the integration and the kind of objects involved. Thus, the esthetic will include those experiences which are truly human, that is, on the level of culture, science, art. These alone can satisfy the human as human.[15]

Religious experience, however, is present even in the face of disturbed conditions. There is effected a higher unification of the self and, as we have seen, it is achieved on the imaginative level between the whole self and the whole universe. The following statement brings out the stable and enduring quality of religious experience.

> . . . this modification of ourselves is enduring. It lasts through any amount of vicissitude of circumstances, internal and external. There is a composing and harmonizing of the various elements of our being such that, in spite of changes in the special conditions that surround us, these conditions are also arranged, settled, in relation to us.[16]

---

[14] *Ibid.*, pp. 17–18.

[15] See *Art as Experience* (New York: G. P. Putnam's Sons, 1934), pp. 58–59. From one point of view, such an integration could be considered to include the whole person, though in comparison with the deeper and more complete harmony of religious experience it is merely "special and partial."

[16] *A Common Faith*, p. 16.

And again:

> Any activity pursued in behalf of an ideal end against obstacles and
> in spite of threats of personal loss because of conviction of its general
> and enduring value is religious in quality.[17]

One more word may be in order regarding our attempt to distinguish
in Dewey's thought between esthetic and religious experience. One may
object on the grounds that such a distinction seems like a dissection and
separation which are alien to his whole theory of experience. It is true,
of course, that for Dewey the increasing perfection of experience could
be said to move horizontally in a continuous line rather than vertically
in separate levels. Hence it may be more correct to speak of "experience," each instance of which contains in varying degrees all the elements which we have considered. Yet whether one talks about difference
of kind or of degree, the "religious" quality of an experience seems to be
of a wider and deeper texture than the "esthetic." [18]

Let us now turn to another aspect of religious experience as envisioned by Dewey. Since it is conceived in terms of an imaginative unification of self with the universe, it is seen that man's complete self-
realization is not an already determined and existing state waiting to
be accomplished. It is not even completely fixed and determined in an
ideal state, as when we would say that a house is determined though
not already existing by reason of the fact that the blueprints have been
completed. Man's self-realization is always in the process of developing,
of being achieved. Dewey uses the example of creation as seen in the
artist, the scientist, the good citizen. It is a creation that is experimental
and continuous which depends on what others have done before and

---

17 *Ibid.*, p. 27.

18 A reason for this difference as seen in Dewey is suggested by Stephen C.
Pepper in an article called "Some Questions on Dewey's Esthetics," *The Philosophy of John Dewey*, ed. Paul Arthur Schilpp, 2nd ed. (New York: Tudor
Publishing Company, 1951), pp. 369–389. Professor Pepper points out two
currents in Dewey's theory of esthetics as seen in *Art as Experience*. The first
current, called the organistic, emphasizes the coherence between an individual
experience and the broader background of experience and the world at large.
The other current, the pragmatic, emphasizes the "had" quality of the experience,
while the sense of coherence and wholeness is secondary and instrumental.
Though Professor Pepper does not discuss religious experience in this article, the
distinction which he makes seems to substantiate the distinction we have de-
tected between religious and esthetic experience. For religious experience emphasizes the sense of wholeness and coherence among experiences, while esthetic
experience emphasizes the "had" quality of the present experience.

are doing now. New values as ends to be achieved are at first dim and uncertain but they grow in shape and definiteness in the process of creation. "The process endures and advances with the life of humanity." [19]

This last point is intimately bound up with Dewey's position on nature and with his rejection of the identification of the religious with the supernatural. It will be recalled that for Dewey nature and man are ongoing. It follows that fixed goals have no place in this framework. By fixed goals he means not only actually existing ones but also those that are ideal but determined—"blocked out," as it were—ahead of time. All goals of this kind are, in his opinion, separated from nature and to assign such goals to man is to separate him from nature. This one-sided view regarding ideals will seem unreasonable to many. It becomes understandable only when it is seen against the background of Dewey's insistence on man's connection with nature.

Thus Dewey is led to the rejection of the supernatural and of all religions which accept the supernatural.[20] In his opinion, every form of the supernatural *by its very nature* is divisive and sets man apart from the world. It does this because it claims "to possess a monopoly of ideals and of the supernatural means by which alone, it is alleged, they can be furthered." [21] In this sense, a religion that is identified with the supernatural is actually destructive of true religious experience as he describes it. It contains an essentially unreligious attitude since it "attributes human achievement and purpose to man in isolation from the world of physical nature and his fellows." [22] Speaking more explicitly of human relations, Dewey states:

> The objection to supernaturalism is that it stands in the way of an effective realization of the sweep and depth of the implications of natural human relations. It stands in the way of using the means that are in our power to make radical changes in these relations. It is certainly true that great material changes might be made with no corresponding improvement of a spiritual or ideal nature. But development in the latter direction cannot be introduced from without; it cannot be brought

---

[19] *A Common Faith*, p. 50.
[20] *A Common Faith* gives other reasons for this rejection. However, one never loses the feeling that these other reasons are brought forward merely to bolster a rejection already made because of the alleged separation of man from nature. This latter is the dominant reason.
[21] *Ibid.*, p. 27.
[22] *Ibid.*, p. 25.

about by dressing up material and economic changes with decorations
derived from the supernatural. It can come only from more intense
realization of values that inhere in the actual connections of human
beings with one another.[23]

Dewey adopts the same position with regard to God. In supernatural
religions, the word "God" means a particular Being with prior and
hence non-ideal existence.[24] This meaning Dewey rejects and for the
same reasons which led him to reject the supernatural. Such a Being is
outside of nature whereas the ideal itself has its roots in natural conditions; "it emerges when the imagination idealizes existence by laying
hold of the possibilities offered to thought and action." [25]

Thus the word "God" means

> this active relation between ideal and actual;[26] . . . the unity of all
> ideal ends arousing us to desire and actions; . . . the ideal ends that
> at a given time and place one acknowledges as having authority over
> his volition and emotions, the values to which one is supremely de-
> voted, as far as these ends, through imagination, take on unity; . . .
> a unification of ideal values that is essentially imaginative in origin
> when the imagination supervenes in conduct.[27]

---

[23] *Ibid.,* p. 80. It would be well at this point to explain what Dewey meant
by "religion" and "supernatural." The meaning of the former word is perhaps
easier to isolate since Dewey defined religion as a "special body of beliefs and
practices having some kind of institutional organization, loose or tight." *A Common Faith,* p. 9. The word "supernatural" is not as easy to define, although it
always refers to that which transcends nature and experience and which consequently not only separates man from nature but also alienates him from it. In
this sense, for Dewey supernatural would mean the same as "transcendental."
However, it is usually restricted to religion as defined above. In any case, in the
following pages the term "supernatural" will be used in Dewey's sense, even
though as used by others it means much more than that.

[24] *Ibid.,* p. 42.

[25] *Ibid.,* p. 48

[26] *Ibid.,* p. 51.

[27] *Ibid.,* pp. 42–43. One may wonder why Dewey was prompted to attempt
an explanation of God since his notion differed so much with the traditional notion. It has been suggested that he did so partly because he did not want to
espouse atheism in a course of lectures on religious themes. Thus, James Oliver
Buswell, Jr., *The Philosophies of F. R. Tennant and John Dewey* (New York:
Philosophical Library, 1950), p. 476, cited by Norbert J. Fleckenstein, M.M.,
*A Critique of John Dewey's Theory of the Nature and the Knowledge of Reality
in the Light of the Principles of Thomism* (Washington, D. C.: The Catholic
University Press, 1954), p. 93. It would seem, however, more plausible to accept
Dewey's own reason for adhering to the term. He wanted to dissociate himself
also from militant atheism which, in his opinion, shares with supernaturalism
the separation of man from nature. In any case, it was the meaning of the term,
not the term itself, that was important. It was this that Dewey was anxious to
set down in precise language.

Dewey, then, was adamant in his opposition to the identification of the religious and the supernatural. Because the latter is destructive of the relations common and natural to man, it weakens and saps the force of the possibilities inherent in such relationships.[28] And because it is destructive of truly religious values, there can be no bridge between these values and supernatural religions.[29]

Dewey's Critique of Religion

The previous discussion has attempted to make clear the importance in Dewey's mind of religious experience as an integrative force, that is, as a condition for the achievement of self-realization. Dewey's development of such experience is continuous with his desire to show how man can seek fulfillment in and through nature. This is so because in a very real sense religious experience itself is continuous with his general theory that experience is simply the achievement of self-realization in the ongoing process of nature. It shares with experience in general the task of enabling the individual to reach wider and deeper unifications of the self with matter. As we have seen, religious experience is distinguished by the fact that it effects a better adjustment in life and its conditions, pertains to our being in its entirety, and is thus more inclusive, deep-seated and enduring, and lasts through all kinds of obstacles, difficulties and threats of personal loss. In this respect, religious experience marks the high point of human development and fulfillment.

In the earlier discussion, we also touched upon the main objections which Dewey raised against institutionalized religion and which led him to make a distinction between "religion" and "religious." Since this distinction is so important for Dewey's whole theory of self-realization and of man's relation to nature, we shall examine these objections more in detail and attempt to show where his position is open to criticism.

For Dewey, that which is fatal for religious experience, as for experience in all its aspects, is the separation of man from the rest of nature. We have seen enough about Dewey's notion of experience to know that his test for the validity of experience and for philosophies of experience is their success in helping man to come to terms with matter.

And this brings us to the main reason why Dewey was so sharply

---

[28] *Ibid.*, p. 27.
[29] *Ibid.*, p. 28.

opposed to institutionalized religions. In his mind they are ineffective as integrating forces because they separate man from nature and thus prevent his self-realization. In fact, religion prevents man from engaging in a truly religious experience.

It would be well now to center attention upon the principal reasons why in Dewey's mind religion separates man from nature. In the main, Dewey's objections may be reduced to two. First, religion proposes separate goals, and second, it is destructive of a sense of "community" and of "social awareness" which is so necessary for self-realization. Each of these will now be examined in turn.

Separate goals. The problem of separate goals in religion is really a specific application of the broad problem of the relation of the ideal and the real, of existence and value, of beliefs about the structure and process of things and the values which should regulate conduct. In Dewey's mind, this is one of the most important problems which man has to face.[30] At the basis of the problem is the supposition that man has a drive toward the achievement of self-realization in and through nature. Further, he must be moved to action by ideals which have their rise in nature and hence are possible for him. There must be no separation between the two.

It is here that Dewey professes to see the most serious weakness of every form of transcendentalism. It proposes for man goals and ideals which are impossible.

> An ideal becomes a synonym for whatever is inspiring—and impossible. Then, since intelligence cannot be wholly suppressed, the ideal is hardened by thought into some high, far-away object. It is so elevated and so distant that it does not belong to this world or to experience. It is in technical language, transcendental, in common speech, supernatural, of heaven not of earth. The ideal is then a goal of final exhaustive, comprehensive perfection which can be defined only by complete contrast with the actual. Although impossible of realization and of conception, it is still regarded as the source of all generous discontent with actualities and of all inspiration to progress.[31]

The impossible ideal professes to inspire intelligent striving on the part of man but then frustrates the work of thought because the object proposed is unobtainable and unrelated to present action and experience.

---

[30] See *The Quest for Certainty* (New York: G. P. Putnam's Sons, 1929), pp. 18–19; *Experience and Nature* (W. W. Norton & Company, Inc., 1929), p. 415; *Reconstruction in Philosophy*, 2nd ed. (Boston: The Beacon Press, 1948), p. 128.

[31] *Human Nature and Conduct*, p. 260.

In other words, Dewey cannot see how ideals as proposed by transcendentalism have relevance to man's concrete situation which is to live in a material universe and to deal with it. For him, transcendentalism does not show the connection between matter and the separate goals which it proposes for man's striving.

The consequences of such a situation, Dewey believes, are evident and disastrous. For one thing, unless man sees clearly the relation of his engagement in the material universe with the goals and ideals proposed, he is left with "an impoverished and truncated experience," [32] and the things of direct experience are degraded.[33] It is no wonder that once matter is deprived of all ideal significance, man becomes a sensualist and materialist of the worst kind. For better or worse, man *must* deal with matter, and as material resources are increasingly exploited, he is becoming more and more concerned with it. If he sees in it only matter and not possibilities of higher significance, his attention will be rooted exclusively in what is sensible and sensual. In this manner, the one who elevates the ideal above and beyond the immediate sense experience acts "like a conspirator with the sensual mind." [34]

It is for this reason that Dewey indicts transcendentalists and spiritual leaders for allying themselves with the sensualist in degrading man to an exclusive concern with the material.

> The final source of the trouble is . . . that the moral and spiritual "leaders" have propagated the notion that ideal ends may be cultivated in isolation from "material" means, as if means and material were not synonymous. While they condemn men for giving to means the thought and energy that ought to go to ends, the condemnation should go to them. For they have not taught their followers to think of material and economic activities as *really* means. They have been unwilling to frame their conception of the values that should be regulative of human conduct on the basis of the actual conditions and operations by which alone values can be actualized.[35]

As an antidote to these alleged defects of transcendentalism, Dewey proposes to find ideals and values in nature itself and in man's dealing

---

[32] *Reconstruction in Philosophy*, p. 101.
[33] *Art as Experience*, p. 31.
[34] *Ibid.*
[35] *The Quest for Certainty*, pp. 280–281. Dewey also states: "The transcendental philosopher has probably done more than the professed sensualist and materialist to obscure the potentialities of daily experience for joy and for self-regulation." *Experience and Nature*, p. 39.

with nature. Thus, his whole theory of esthetic and religious experience takes on new dimensions. For it is nothing more than a hymn of praise of and confidence in the possibilities of concrete experience to help man achieve his fulfillment. In his opinion, one *can* and indeed *must* find self-realization in the context of concrete, human experience, in the interaction between man and his environment. This approach will restore in man his respect for matter and for ideals which should be the activating force of action.

> To respect matter means to respect the conditions of achievement; conditions which hinder and obstruct and which have to be changed, conditions which help and further and which can be used to modify obstructions and attain ends. Only as men have learned to pay sincere and persistent regard to matter, to the conditions upon which depends negatively and positively the success of all endeavor, have they shown sincere and fruitful respect for ends and purposes.[36]

For Dewey, interest in the material universe, especially in the industrial and technological form it now assumes, can lead to materialism of the worst kind. However, this would be true only if such an outlook "reflected and reported the chief features of the existing situation as if they were final, without regard to what they may become.[37] But he felt that his theory of esthetic and religious experience had forestalled that possibility and had opened up to man the whole realm of ideals and values which had been blocked by transcendentalism.

Dewey develops the same theme from a different viewpoint. He speaks about the relative efficacy of separate *vs.* natural goals as motivating forces for action. In his mind, to remove ends, goals and ideals to a separate place outside of nature is to deprive them of their power to stimulate man to engage in furthering the ongoing processes of nature. Such ideals become ineffective as incentives for action. Dewey is insistent on this point. He intends it to apply not only to goals that are outside nature and non-existent, that is, yet to be brought into being, but also to outside goals which are existent but yet to be achieved. For him, the only goals that have power to activate man so that he will participate in the development of nature are those that are non-existent but to be achieved in and through nature. The following statement illustrates his position regarding ideals which are efficacious as motivating forces.

---

[36] *Reconstruction in Philosophy*, p. 72.
[37] *The Quest for Certainty*, p. 79.

For all endeavor for the better is moved by faith in what is possible, not by adherence to the actual. Nor does this faith depend for its moving power upon intellectual assurance or belief that the things worked for must surely prevail and come into embodied existence. For the authority of the object to determine our attitude and conduct, the right that is given it to claim our allegiance and devotion is based on the intrinsic nature of the ideal.[38]

Dewey consequently maintains that only possible, non-existent goals are the most "real," that is, most capable of moving us to action. For "the reality of ideal ends as ideals is vouched for by their undeniable power in action." [39] And, of course, by ideal ends he means ends that are possible and as yet non-existent. He further states:

The reality of ideal ends and values in their authority over us is an undoubted fact. The validity of justice, affection, and that intellectual correspondence of our ideas with realities that we call truth is so assured in its hold upon humanity that it is unnecessary for the religious attitude to encumber itself with the apparatus of dogma and doctrine.[40]

The only thing that objects of religion can add to their motivating efficacy is the force of punishment and reward.[41]

There is another characteristic of separate goals which, in Dewey's opinion, deprives them of motivating power. It is the fact that belief in such goals reserved for another world can be an excuse for retiring into a life of inactivity. When the evils of this world become overburdening, one can console himself in the thought that after this life one can retire to a place of happiness and peace. It frees him from the responsibility of coming to grips with the problems of human living. Thought of another world becomes a refuge and not a resource.[42] Or one can assure himself that in spite of everything the transcendent Being will finally make all turn out for the best. Dewey charges this viewpoint with injecting into man a lazy complacency, depriving him of the manliness and courage to engage himself in directing natural and social ends for the good of mankind.[43] To talk of absolutes in terms that indicate existent and assured goals is to engage in the worst kind of egotism, sentimentalism and optimism.[44]

---

[38] *A Common Faith,* p. 23.
[39] *Ibid.,* p. 43.
[40] *Ibid.,* p. 44.
[41] *Ibid.*
[42] *The Quest for Certainty,* p. 306.
[43] *A Common Faith,* p. 24.
[44] *Ibid.,* pp. 25, 46.

Sense of Community, Social Awareness. The previous section treated in its broader and more general phase the failure of religion as an integrative force in man's life, for it dealt with the separation of man from his environment at large. This section will discuss the more particular aspect of the environment, where environment now means the community of people in which man must find his self-realization. Specifically, Dewey raises the objection that religion is disruptive of the sense of community, of social awareness, without which man cannot achieve fulfillment.

The importance of the communal aspect of man has been discussed in previous chapters.[45] Dewey insists on the necessity of shared goals and on the use of shared means for the attainment of those goals. He stresses the fact that man must assume a sense of responsibility in attempting to improve the human estate in order that he may achieve a degree of economic and social security without which man cannot attain esthetic and religious experience, that is, self-realization.

At the outset, Dewey's view of traditional religion is dominated by the opinion that it is individualistically oriented since it is chiefly concerned with the salvation of the isolated individual soul. Such an orientation destroys at its root the ability of religion to act as an integrative force for it prevents the individual from achieving the sense of wholeness which is so necessary for self-realization. This sense of wholeness cannot be achieved by developing it in the individual first and then extending it to form a unified society. This is sheer fantasy. The only way to attain this sense of wholeness and to sustain it in existence is to do so "through membership in a society which has attained a degree of unity." [46] In this sense, "religion is not so much a root of unity as it is its flower or fruit." [47]

What Dewey is equivalently saying is that religion cannot be an integrative force because it is essentially individualistic. One must first find integration, a sense of wholeness, by engaging in community life, that is, in the pursuit of shared goals which are discovered independently of religion. Once this sense of community is attained, one will be put in contact, not with religion, but with *religious experience.*

Dewey's theory of morals is in accord with this theory. He suggests

---

[45] *Supra*, chaps. IV–V.
[46] *Individualism Old and New*, p. 64.
[47] *Ibid.*

that the individualistic orientation of traditional religion accounts for the restriction of morals to individual conduct. He then states:

> The idea that the stable and expanding institution of all things that make life worth while throughout all human relationships is the real object of all intelligent conduct is depressed from view by the current conception of morals as a special kind of action chiefly concerned with either the virtues or the enjoyments of individuals in their personal capacities.[48]

Dewey does not hesitate to address himself to the implications of such an orientation. He equates it with the idea of *laissez faire* in politics and economics. The root of *laissez faire* is "denial (more often implicit than express) of the possibility of radical intervention of intelligence in the conduct of human life." [49] In religion, it leads to the abandonment of all hope of human intervention in the direction of events for the achievement of social improvement.[50] Religion thus "stands in the way of an effective realization of the sweep and depth of the implications of natural human relations. It stands in the way of using the means that are in our power to make radical changes in these relations." [51] The only solution is to steep oneself intensely in the onward movement of human events and to direct them through intelligence to the betterment of the human estate.

For Dewey, then, man must choose between two alternatives. He must depend either upon the supernatural with its depreciation of natural intelligence, knowledge and understanding, or upon human agencies with their confidence in these natural resources.[52] Dewey leaves no doubt as to which choice must be that of all men sincerely interested in furthering the ongoing process of nature.

In all this, Dewey has great confidence in man's sense of solidarity with his fellow man and in his natural impulses to affection, compassion and justice, equality and freedom both for himself and for others. He feels sure that these impulses will inspire man to labor for the attainment of such natural advantages.[53] All that is needed is to unify these aspirations so that the objects to which they are directed may be

---

48 *The Quest for Certainty*, pp. 31–32.
49 *A Common Faith*, p. 78.
50 *Ibid.*
51 *Ibid.*, p. 80.
52 *Ibid.*, p. 80.
53 *Ibid.*, p. 81.

more effectively achieved. It is in this connection that he ends his book
on religious experience with the following resounding paragraph.

> The considerations put forward in the present chapter may be summed
> up in what they imply. The ideal ends to which we attach our faith
> are not shadowy and wavering. They assume concrete form in our
> understanding of our relations to one another and the values contained
> in these relations. We who now live are parts of a humanity that ex-
> tends into the remote past, a humanity that has interacted with nature.
> The things in civilization we most prize are not of ourselves. They
> exist by grace of the doings and sufferings of the continuous human
> community in which we are a link. Ours is the responsibility of con-
> serving, transmitting, rectifying and expanding the heritage of values
> we have received that those who come after us may receive it more
> solid and secure, more widely accessible and more generously shared
> than we have received it. Here are all the elements for a religious faith
> that shall not be confined to sect, class, or race. Such a faith has always
> been implicitly the common faith of mankind. It remains to make it
> explicit and militant.[54]

Evaluation of Dewey's Critique

With religious experience, we have arrived at the most important element of Dewey's thought, for on it depends the meaning of experience
on all levels. Every genuine experience, even the most casual and ordinary, must include at least an implicit awareness of the extensive and
underlying whole. Without it, an experience is "torn from the common
context" and "stands alone and isolated." It marks the difference between sanity and madness.

For the same reason, Dewey's whole theory of self-realization is bound
up with religious experience. For in the last analysis, one achieves self-
realization only when he somehow sees the meaning of the present
moment and activity in the context of the expanding possibilities of an
indefinite future. Upon religious experience, too, depend the validity
and value of Dewey's work in more specialized fields, that is, in art, science, education, politics, social theory, ethics, and even logic. For in
these fields he is attempting to work out specific conditions according
to which the human personality may achieve the highest possible degree of self-realization and this, in turn, consists in religious experience.

---

[54] *Ibid.,* p. 87.

Lastly, if all this is so, on religious experience will depend whatever influence America will have on the rest of the world. As we have seen, the problems which Dewey has faced are, in his opinion, "the problems of the world." And the solution of these problems has been framed in terms of his theory of experience, especially of religious experience. It is in these terms that America is to pay back its debt to Europe by helping to solve new problems in new ways.

From all this it can be seen how important is Dewey's theory of religious experience. It must bear the burden not only of America but of the world. It has set for itself a high purpose, it has engendered high hopes. More than any other element in his philosophy, religious experience will be the criterion for the formation of a judgment as to whether Dewey's philosophy, and indeed many forms of American naturalism, will stand the test of time.

It is important, then, that any consideration of his thought should include a more detailed evaluation of his theory of religious experience. This evaluation will have a twofold purpose. One will be to underscore the limitations of such a theory; limitations which, if not adjusted, will undermine all that he has to say. But such an evaluation will not be merely negative. It will also serve to show how one can retain the fruitful elements of his thought. With this in mind, we may now move on to an evaluation of Dewey's criticism of religion. In doing this, we shall follow the order of topics as treated in the preceding pages.

Separate goals. What precisely is the goal which Dewey proposes? It follows from his whole theory of experience. Man is seen to be engaged in a series of losses and recoveries of equilibrium in which series the same *individual* is for the most part involved. On the higher levels of experience, however, namely, the esthetic and religious, the individual stretches out to a whole which consists in the imaginative unification and projection of all the possibilities existing in man and in the universe. It is a goal which never will be completely achieved by an individual, nor even by all of humanity, at any one time, simply because the goal is not a limit that is eventually approached and attained. The most that one can do is to accept the goods of life that have been handed down by previous ages and pass them on, improved and developed, to succeeding ages.

Moreover, it is this unification of possibilities for a limitless future that gives the individual a sense of being founded on a rock with the consequent feeling of stability and peace. In this, too, man attains a solidarity with the whole human race of which he is a part and gains satisfaction in the knowledge that he is contributing to the ongoing process of humanity. Self-realization, had at the present moment, consists in the completion that one experiences when he contributes to the betterment of future generations.

At first glance, this ideal appears to be a powerful and inspiring one, and in many respects it is. But serious difficulties arise. For the goal is not something accurately defined nor is the time of achievement definitely placed. The goal is a process, growing and developing, but never completed.[55] The person, or better, humanity, is on the way, but never arriving. Although man may find completions in a given limited series of disorientations and re-integrations, he finds his deepest satisfaction by stretching out to an indefinite, limitless whole. But what is this whole? It is an "imaginative and projected unification" of expanding possibilities which is ever in the process of being organized. We do not know what form it will take; it will have to be shaped and reshaped, tentatively stated and revised. One can never say at any moment whether or not it is accurately formulated, for tomorrow may dictate a change.

Furthermore, besides the fact that the goal itself is ill-defined, it is not the individual, or any group of individuals, who attains the goal, but some faceless whole. Though the individual may attain periodic and limited completions in the course of his life, his deepest satisfaction seems to consist in bettering the lot of future, nameless individuals. One wonders whether Dewey is not straining selflessness a bit. For if extended too far, the concept "selfless" will begin to mean exactly what it says and will negate the whole concept of "self-realization." No matter how much we may stress altruism, there must be an element of "selfishness" involved in the sense that the self cannot be completely blotted out of the picture. From all this it follows that Dewey's goal labors under the very difficulty which he professed to see in transcendentalism, namely, it is impossible of attainment.

To the weight of these difficulties is added Dewey's view with regard to man's future. The universe may slay us and humanity itself is "but a slight and feeble thing, perhaps an episodic one, in the vast stretch of the universe." [56] More specifically, he would certainly say that the

---

[55] *Human Nature and Conduct*, p. 282.

[56] *The Public and Its Problems* (New York: Holt, Rinehart & Winston, Inc., 1927), p. 176.

life of the individual ceases with the grave. The challenging cry of "still we may trust" suddenly becomes weak and thin.

In the light of these difficulties, the possibility of achieving self-realization becomes highly questionable. For it is a consummation which is achieved *now*. On the highest level of religious experience the individual is supposed to reach a sense of inner peace and harmony which unites all the disparate elements of his life into a unified whole, giving them meaning. Also, this inner peace must endure in the face of all kinds of obstacles, both interior and exterior. Yet, in view of the vagueness of the goal, the uncertainty of its achievement and the inevitable destruction of the individual, experience is stillborn. It is incapable of being viable in the face of the difficulties confronting it. It is too much to ask that the vitality of a present experience depend upon a destructive future. Dewey has indeed said that "the good is now or never." [57] It is to be feared that such a statement can be looked upon as an expression of despair rather than of hope.

Again, Dewey had argued that transcendental goals are powerless to move the individual to action. But what has been said regarding the vagueness and indefiniteness of the goal proposed by Dewey tends to undermine its own motivating power. Such goals would offer inadequate motivation even to "manliness, courage and responsibility," especially in time of difficulty. Man is motivated to action more by the concrete and well-defined than by the vague and indefinite.[58]

This has important consequences for Dewey's indictment of transcendental goals. He had said that they do not show man the value of involvement in matter. This failure would lead man to give up hope of deriving values from matter with the result that in discouragement he will turn back to matter with a vengeance. But if the goal of naturalism is inadequate, it, too, will be unable to prevent such a situation. The return to matter and immersion in it will be even more complete since naturalism has removed the restraints supplied by the notion of sin which results from the inordinate dealing with matter. On his own

---

[57] *Human Nature and Conduct,* p. 290.

[58] So far in our response to Dewey's objections against religion, we have omitted what is perhaps the most important one for Dewey, namely, the objection that religion presents goals which transcend human experience and hence are impossible. Since an answer to this objection requires a discussion of other aspects of Dewey's naturalism, it will be reserved for the next chapter which deals with the notion of community, "wholeness" and "onward thrust of experience and nature."

terms, naturalism is seen to be no better than transcendentalism. It is in fact worse, since it has more difficulties and fewer benefits.

Sense of Community, Social Awareness. Dewey's objection that religion is essentially individualistic and hence disruptive of community life seems largely to have been influenced by the "divisions and separations" and the "inward laceration" which he experienced during his early New England days.[59] But this objection seems to be entirely too sweeping and all-inclusive. It may be true that one or other religion emphasizes interest in one's own welfare to the exclusion of others. But institutionalized Christian religions generally look upon such orientations as aberrations rather than as an authentic spirit. The "love thy neighbor" of the gospel has been the inspiration for altruism of a high order and has evoked instances of heroism in self-sacrifice for one's fellow man. In fact, one may say that love as a genuine virtue was introduced into western culture only with the advent of Christianity.

In addition, one may point out weaknesses in Dewey's own notion of community. It is his contention that man has impulses to affection, compassion, justice, and so on. These will move him to action in contributing to the ongoing process of humanity. Certainly no one will deny the presence to some degree of such impulses. To do so would be overly pessimistic. But this does not justify the opposite extreme. Man has corresponding impulses to selfishness and greed, putting man in conflict with himself and with the rest of humanity. Even in the best of situations, man finds himself pulled in two directions. The situation becomes more acute when he is presented with goals which are badly formulated and which do not meet his deep-seated drive to find personal fulfillment.

At the root of the above difficulties is another deficiency in Dewey's whole theory of self-realization and of community. It is his failure to work out an adequate theory of love.[60] It is true that Dewey stressed

59 "From Absolutism to Experimentalism," *Contemporary American Philosophy,* eds. George P. Adams and Wm. Pepperell Montague (New York: The Macmillan Company, 1930), II, 19.

60 It cannot be denied that love is implicit in Dewey's thought. But so important is it that it should receive explicit attention. We shall attempt to outline the main points of such a treatment and to indicate the weaknesses of Dewey's position. For a fuller treatment of love—of God, of self and of neighbor—see: Pierre Rousselot, S.J., *Pour l'histoire du problème de l'amour au moyen âge* (Paris: J. Vrin, 1933); Louis-B. Geiger, *Le problème de l'amour chez Saint Thomas d'Aquin* (Paris: J. Vrin, 1952); Robert O. Johann, S.J., *The Meaning of Love* (Westminster: The Newman Press, 1955); M. C. D'Arcy, S.J., *The Mind and Heart of Love* (New York: Holt, Rinehart & Winston, Inc., 1947).

the need of interpersonal relationships in order that man may reach
fulfillment. In this orientation, he has made an important contribution
to a theory of man and of self-realization. He has shown that human
development and fulfillment cannot be achieved by man in isolation.
From this point of view, his philosophy is decidedly "social" in character.
In this, he is in accord with modern theories of personality. Thus, in
speaking of the characteristics of a mature personality, Gordon W. Allport, in his classic work on Personality, states:

> In the first place, the developed person is one who has a variety of
> autonomous interests; that is, he can lose himself in work, in contem-
> plation, in recreation, and in loyalty to others. He participates with
> warmth and vigor in whatever pursuits have for him acquired value.
> Egocentricity is not the mark of a mature personality . . . Paradoxi-
> cally, 'self-expression' requires the capacity to lose oneself in the pur-
> suit of objectives, not primarily referred to the self. Unless directed
> outward toward socialized and culturally compatible ends, unless ab-
> sorbed in causes and goals that outshine self-seeking and vanity, any
> life seems dwarfed and immature.[61]

Compare this with the following statement of Dewey:

> The kind of self which is formed through action which is faithful to
> relations with others will be a fuller and broader self than one which
> is cultivated in isolation from or in opposition to the purposes and
> needs of others. In contrast, the kind of self which results from gen-
> erous breadth of interest may be said alone to constitute a develop-
> ment and fulfillment of self, while the other way of life stunts and
> starves selfhood by cutting it off from connections necessary to its
> growth.[62]

Yet, in giving emphasis to a community of selves, Dewey has slighted
the intensely personal and fruitful relationship of self to self. There is
little explicit treatment of love, self-donation, the going out of one

---

[61] *Personality: A Psychological Interpretation* (New York: Holt, Rinehart &
Winston, Inc., 1937), p. 213.

[62] *Ethics*, 2nd ed. rev. (New York: Holt, Rinehart & Winston, Inc., 1932),
p. 335. Several points should be added here. First, Allport, too, despite his classic
analysis of personality, gives very little explicit treatment of love as a factor in
personality development; one page, in fact, sc. p. 217. Second, in comparing
Dewey and Allport we do not intend to imply that they are in complete agreement in their approach to psychology. See, for example, the criticism of Dewey
by Allport in the Schilpp edition, pp. 263–290, and Dewey's reply, pp. 554–556.
For a development of the importance of love from a psychological viewpoint, see
Smiley Blanton, M.D., *Love or Perish* (New York: Simon and Schuster, Inc.,
1956).

individual to another. Jean Mouroux has pointed out that a person is never himself except insofar as he gives himself, links himself with another person as with another self.[63] But this giving is not a complete emptying of self; rather the other person comes "to enrich his being, fulfil his aspiration, and set his inner impulse free." [64] Love is seen as an integrative force by which a person finds fulfillment.[65]

From one point of view, perhaps, it would seem that too much emphasis should not be given to this weakness in Dewey's thought. Though one would like to see a more explicit treatment of love, Dewey would certainly take his stand with those who would rather experience love than be able to define it. But there is another very important consequence involved. It is this: Even if Dewey had given a more conscious formulation of love as an integrating factor, love would still be inadequate within a purely naturalistic framework. Dewey's theory of religious experience necessarily demands that the individual see the implications of his activity for future generations. If love is included here, it means that the individual must go out in love to innumerable faceless and nameless individuals and that he labor strenuously for their sakes. In fact, it is the awareness that one is somehow contributing to the betterment of unknown people that gives the present moment its meaning and fulfillment, "through any amount of vicissitude of circumstances, internal and external," "against obstacles and in spite of threats of personal loss." But how can one encompass in his love countless unknown individuals? Human love is limited and demands a higher unification if it is to radiate in unlimited directions and shed its light and warmth in unlimited degrees. Naturalism is inadequate to meet the challenge and from this aspect, too, a naturalistic theory of religious experience is stillborn. In the following chapter an attempt will be made to show how a theory of love, and a theory of community, can be extended to answer this difficulty.

---

[63] Jean Mouroux, *The Meaning of Man,* trans. A. H. G. Downes (New York: Sheed & Ward, 1952), p. 207.

[64] *Ibid.,* p. 203.

[65] "Love brings growth in being. It reveals men to themselves. It seeks them out in their intimate depths to set their energies free, to answer their deepest call, to find their still veiled and ambiguous meaning and bring it to light." *Ibid.,* p. 207.

Conclusion

Dewey's naturalism eliminated the transcendental as an integrating factor in man's effort to achieve self-realization. He felt that his theory of esthetic and religious experience would give meaning to human situations and events. It cannot be denied that he has brought forward some insights which will help to raise many aspects of life above the level of dull routine, rescue them from mere drudgery and prevent the depersonalization of man. But has his position adequately faced the more pressing problems of human existence? The universe with which man has to deal is recalcitrant, stubborn, often destructive. There are times when it will bring man to his knees in sorrow and frustration. Is his theory able to overcome those situations where man, in spite of every effort to the contrary, is forced by circumstances to undergo the painful drudgery of hard and laborious toil? What is he to do in these situations? What is to sustain man? Indeed, what is to give meaning to the universe in all its aspects?

These are questions which Dewey has not adequately answered. He has taken his stand with those who look with impatience upon the so-called "problem of evil." He has admitted that indeed the world may yet rise to slay us. But in spite of the fact that he seeks to refute the problem largely by ignoring it, it stands there demanding an answer and asserting that unless the answer is given, all attempts to work out the conditions for human self-realization will end in failure.

For Dewey, to appeal to a future life and to an Absolute is to manifest weakness and sentimentality, to seek a refuge of consolation and solace as a last resort for sorrow, to withdraw from the ongoing process of nature and thus to destroy any hope of self-realization. That the doctrine of evil and of a future life can be all of these things, no one will deny. But it need not be so. Such positions can be looked upon as existential facts which confront man and help to shed light on areas of human experience which are hopelessly unintelligible in any other framework. And if at the same time these positions do *not* withdraw man from engagement in the world, then they give meaning, hope and encouragement so that one may go on to engage manfully in the processes of nature. In this, man can reach fulfillment even amid onerous tasks; even, one might say, amid the assembly-line work of a modern factory.

Thus there are times when the onerous aspect of life's situations becomes imperious and all but absorbs our entire attention. A naturalistic framework can help to lift one's mind somewhat from the situation at hand to higher meanings. But the goals it proposes are inadequate to provide a complete solution. In the face of such situations, for a large part of suffering humanity frustration is inevitable unless the things of the universe are linked to something more real and positive than non-existent ideals and a vague hope in a better humanity for the future.

VII   FURTHER ASPECTS OF DEWEY'S NATURALISM

It has often been said that old opinions die hard. Hence it should not be surprising that during the period of over twenty-five years since John Dewey's book on religion, *A Common Faith,* first appeared,[1] some have refused to believe that he seriously intended to reject completely the traditional notions of God and religion. Justification for this refusal is sought especially in the fact that he actually used the word "God," and even attempted a definition of it.

Corliss Lamont reviews this question [2] and rejects the position of those who would classify Dewey as a convert to theism, or who would try to maintain that he believed in a God as some impersonal process in nature, or that he developed a theology. It is his contention also that Dewey did not recognize any power other than ourselves which concerns itself with furthering man's effort to actualize ideal ends; that he did not bring into his system a naturalistic interpretation of deity; that he limited himself to creative human intelligence, using scientific laws and techniques in dealing with the processes of nature; that he believed the cosmos as a whole to be neutral regarding human aims and values.

Professor Lamont draws some conclusions regarding Dewey's use of the term "God." Though Dewey suggested that the term *may* be used to sum up man's activities in actualizing the totality of human ideals, he held that each individual must decide for himself whether he wishes to adopt this redefinition of God. Dewey himself did not incorporate the word into his "common faith" or into his philosophy. "John Dewey

---

[1] New Haven: Yale University Press, 1934.
[2] "New Light on Dewey's *Common Faith,*" *Journal of Philosophy,* LVIII (1961), 21–28.

was not, then, in any sense a theist, but an uncompromising naturalist or humanist thinker." [3]

One cannot help but commend Professor Lamont for the clarity with which he has focused attention upon some of the main issues involved in any evaluation of Dewey's naturalism. One must also agree with him when he criticizes the exaggerations of those who, approaching Dewey from their own position, attempt to bring him into the camp of theism. However, equally subject to criticism is the procedure of those who, from their own position, press hard the naturalistic elements of his thought to the exclusion of other insights.

Certainly there can be no denying the fact that, as far as his *explicit* formulations are concerned, Dewey excluded the transcendental from his philosophy. At the basis of his naturalism is his insistence on man's continuity with nature and on the fact that man can achieve self-realization only in and through nature. For this reason Dewey excluded all forms of the transcendental, the Absolute, God, simply because, in his opinion, they separate man from nature and deprive him of all possibility of reaching self-realization through the development of natural capacities.

It is in this sense, and in this sense alone, that his philosophy and the world with which it was concerned can be called "closed." It is important to understand the proper meaning of this term. It is one which Dewey abhorred, for just as his world was an open and growing world in which novelty abounds, so his philosophy was open and growing with the growing changes in the universe. When we say, therefore, that the world and his philosophy about the world were "closed," we mean that he did not admit anything beyond the forces of nature. It is in this sense that he adopts the position of a thoroughgoing naturalist.

So much can be said of Dewey's *explicit* statements. But are there *implicit* elements in his philosophy which indicate that it is not as thoroughly naturalistic as many of his followers would maintain? What is meant here is that certain elements of his thought, in spite of his explicit statements, were already on the way to breaking out of the narrow limitations placed on them. One might say that his thought, like everything else, was in "process," growing, developing, sometimes "projecting," even saying, more than was explicitly intended.

But perhaps to some who will consider as too subtle the distinction

---

[3] *Ibid.*, p. 25.

made between Dewey's explicit and implicit formulations, the fore-going position may seem too strong. It may give the appearance of at-tempting to "smuggle" an Absolute into his thought, to bring him into the camp of theism. Let us restate the position in a more modified form as follows. *At the very least*, Dewey's theory of experience, *from within*, is capable of, presents no obstacle to, being extended, *even to a transcendental*, by one who adopts this basic notion of experience and who places himself within its framework. Only the main lines of this procedure will be given, for a full development would require another book. In any case, from this viewpoint what Dewey said or meant to say is not nearly as important as that to which his thought can lead.

Three aspects of Dewey's thought will be discussed. The first is his notion of community. The other two I have chosen to call "the sense of wholeness" and "the onward thrust of experience and nature."

The Notion of Community

In the preceding chapter, we examined Dewey's notion of community and pointed out what we thought to be inadequacies. The main objec-tion was that a naturalistic theory of love is too limited to sustain re-ligious experience as he envisioned it. It must be extended. Actually, Dewey could have done this from the standpoint of evolution.[4] He concurs with the judgment of his contemporaries that the universe is literally an evolution. The world of objects has developed from inor-ganic matter to living beings. These, in turn, have gone through suc-cessive stages of perfection, producing organisms with more complicated ways of interacting with the environment—plants, animals and finally man. The latter stands on the peak of the evolutionary process and into his hands has been committed in large measure the future course of evolution. In fact, we might say that in man evolution has become con-scious of itself.[5]

When evolution reaches man, it ceases to be merely biological and

---

[4] This standpoint is developed by Bruno de Solages, "Christianity and Evolu-tion," *Cross Currents*, I (1951), 26–37. The original French article appeared as "La pensée chrétienne face à l'évolution," *Bulletin de littérature ecclesiastique*, XLVIII (1947), ciii–cxvi.

[5] This phrase seems to have been coined by Julian Huxley. See his introduction to Pierre Teilhard de Chardin, *The Phenomenon of Man*, trans. Bernard Wall (New York: Harper & Row, Publishers, 1959), p. 20.

becomes social.[6] This means that there develops a human community which unifies persons with due respect for individual personalities. In Dewey's terms, man develops by reaching full unification and realization through living in the human community where everyone is united by shared goals and by shared means to the attainment of those goals.

But what force is strong enough to achieve this delicate balance where individuals are to develop while at the same time they respect the opportunities of others for developing their own potentialities? This force is love; and not love for countless people, which is impossible, nor for an undifferentiated mass, which is meaningless. The love demanded must receive a higher unification in a transcendent being who is personal and capable of eliciting love of humans not only for himself but for one another. In this regard, de Solages writes:

> How can we unify persons in a great human community which would nevertheless respect their personalities? What force would be strong enough, yet delicate enough for this higher synthesis of spirits? This force could only be love. But love is something eminently personal. It is the intimate relation of Thou and I. How could we be capable of loving directly with a real love billions of other persons, to whom the evolution of the universe has given birth? It would seem that humanity could not achieve this synthesis of communion in love except indirectly, by uniting itself about a superpersonal center which is strong enough to love the multitude of spirits, a superpersonal center which would unite them in its love by making them superpersonal. *The forward progress of humanity* (at present the last stage of the evolution of the Universe) *can never be achieved except by love of God.* But this can never happen—and, now we are at this point, we perceive that the whole previous movement of evolution is otherwise inconceivable—unless God be not a point of ideal projections, but a real and present center of attraction, whose force is felt from the very beginning of evolution, and therefore a *transcendent center* to evolution.[7]

From this viewpoint, a transcendent being is seen to unify experience on a higher level, namely, that of love. Human love with such a basis becomes an integrative force in one's life. Having roots in a communion of love that is ultimately oriented to a superpersonal center, it calls forth a response on the part of each individual. It fulfills the deepest longing of the human spirit to reach outside itself and dissolve

---

[6] de Saloges, *loc. cit.*, p. 33.
[7] *Ibid.*, pp. 34–35.

its inner isolation. It expands and enriches the lover. It releases energies by providing an adequate motive for action and gives purpose and direction to energies thus released. It transcends physical beauty or ugliness and helps the individual to go beyond likes and dislikes based on externals. It consequently provides the only adequate antidote for selfishness, for it alone gives a satisfactory reason for being concerned with one's fellow man and for expending one's energies in his behalf without at the same time emptying the individual. If understood in this way, love will be a powerful force inspiring man to concern himself with nature and matter as means of achieving those goals which are necessary for the betterment of mankind.

From all this, it should be clear that God is infinitely more than a "rewarder and avenger." He is a Person to Whom one can give himself and in the giving find the fulfillment of all his aspirations. Moreover, to God, a separate goal, must be ultimately attributed the reason why human beings are lovable in themselves with all the consequent enrichment of the lover and the resulting involvement in human affairs and events. In fact, as we have noted, such a separate goal is the only adequate motive for interest in our fellow man. Lastly, this approach to goals is the only remedy for a corroding selfishness and the one firm foundation for a real community. Seen in this light, God is not "separate" at all. Rather He is "present to," "immanent in," nature and experience. It is precisely His transcendence that makes His immanence more meaningful for human self-realization.

The Sense of Wholeness

That which is characteristic of an experience, even of the most casual and ordinary kind, is its unifying quality. This quality unifies disparate elements to form a single experience and likewise makes for continuity among experiences. It furthermore links every individual experience with an indefinite whole which gives meaning to the experience, "for the mad, the insane, thing to us is that which is torn from the common context and which stands alone and isloated," [8] and "without an indeterminate and undetermined setting, the material of any experience is incoherent." [9] The individual has the sense of belonging to an in-

---

[8] *Art as Experience* (New York: G. P. Putnam's Sons, 1934), p. 194.
[9] *Ibid.*, p. 195.

definite whole which moves as he moves, which he can never adequately encompass.

This sense of wholeness is especially felt on the deeper levels of esthetic and religious experience. It reaches its culmination on the most profound level of religious experience where the sense of wholeness gives us a feeling of inner peace and harmony which endures in the face of internal and external vicissitudes. In spite of the changes that occur in the special conditions surrounding us, we maintain an inward sense of settlement. We feel as though we are founded on a rock and no amount of obstacles or threats of personal loss can shake this inner harmony.[10]

This union with an indefinite whole also explains the meaning of every striving and of every action. When speaking about ideals as guides of action, Dewey attempts to show that in every particular aim selected there is a sense of an indefinite context of consequences and it is from among these that the particular aim is chosen.

> For the sense of an indefinite context of consequences from among which the aim is selected enters into the *present* meaning of activity. The "end" is the figured pattern at the center of the field through which runs the axis of conduct. About this central figuration extends infinitely a supporting background in a vague whole, undefined and undiscriminated.[11]

Intelligence focuses on that one little part of the whole which is the axis of movement. The other consequences, both collateral and remote, are only vaguely and dimly grasped through a background of feeling or of diffused emotion.

> In a genuine sense every act is already possessed of infinite import. The little part of the scheme of affairs which is modifiable by our efforts is continuous with the rest of the world . . . When a sense of the infinite reach of an act physically occurring in a small point of space and occupying a petty instant of times comes home to us, the *meaning* of the present act is seen to be vast, immeasurable, unthinkable.[12]

This whole which is so important for human experience consists of an ideal, that is, an imaginative projection of all the possibilities of development both for the self and for the material world. It includes

---

[10] All of this has already been discussed. See chap. VI.

[11] *Human Nature and Conduct* (New York: Holt, Rinehart & Winston, Inc., 1922), p. 262.

[12] *Ibid.*, pp. 262–263.

all the things that can come into existence through the interaction of man with environing conditions. The *whole* self means all the possibilities for development of human capacities. The same may be said of the *whole* world, or Universe, as Dewey calls it. The Universe is the totality of all possible conditions with which the self may be connected.[13] Combining both man and the Universe, Dewey gives an extended definition of Nature.

> Nature signifies nothing less than the whole complex of the results of the interaction of man, with his memories and hopes, understanding and desire, with that world to which one-sided philosophy confines "nature." [14]

This sense of wholeness, then, is that which gives meaning to experience, or more precisely, to the consummatory stage of experience. Since this is so, the connection between the sense of wholeness and self-realization is evident, for the latter is nothing else but the achievement of consummation and satisfaction in varying degrees. It is this stretching out to infinity which gives meaning to every experience from the most ordinary to esthetic and religious experience and hence it gives meaning to self-realization itself. The individual is aware not only of what he is but also of what he might become. In fact, it is this keen awareness of what he might become that gives meaning to the present moment. For "we are carried out beyond ourselves to find ourselves; . . . the whole is felt as an expansion of ourselves; . . . we are citizens of this vast world beyond ourselves." [15]

We see that Dewey is deeply imbued with the feeling that man is constantly reaching out to what is beyond. He recognized that it was not something that man could control, that he could handle intellectually.[16] It is an emotional experience which must not, however, be equated with "emotionalism." It is something that man cannot shake off, or perhaps that man shakes off only to his own detriment so that his personality becomes isolated and stunted. But Dewey was convinced that, if the individual gives in to it, the sense of the abiding whole beyond the confines of our immediate environment will lead to man's deepest fulfillment and realization.

It is in this aspect of experience that Dewey's thought shows the in-

---

13 *A Common Faith,* p. 19.
14 *Art as Experience,* p. 152.
15 *Ibid.,* p. 195.
16 *Human Nature and Conduct,* p. 263; *A Common Faith,* p. 19.

fluence of Hegel. Dewey's attraction to Hegel in his early philosophical work is a familiar story and needs no lengthy treatment now.[17] Nor is there any doubt that the Absolute Mind of Hegelianism collapsed before the inroads which evolution and the New Psychology made upon his own thought. But we have, I think, a clue to the origin of the elements which we have been discussing in his statement of one of the reasons for the appeal that Hegel's thought made to him.

> . . . it supplied a demand for unification that was doubtless an intense emotional craving, and yet was a hunger that only an intellectualized subject-matter could satisfy. It is more than difficult, it is impossible, to recover that early mood. But the sense of divisions and separations that were, I suppose, borne in upon me as a consequence of a heritage of New England culture, divisions by way of isolation of self from the world, of soul from body, of nature from God, brought a painful oppression—or, rather, they were an inward laceration . . . Hegel's synthesis of subject and object, matter and spirit, the divine and the human, was, however, no mere intellectual formula; it operated as an immense release, a liberation. Hegel's treatment of human culture, of institutions and the arts, involved the same dissolution of hard-and-fast dividing walls, and had a special attraction for me.[18]

Dewey never lost this demand for unification. He himself admitted a lasting influence of and appreciation for Hegel.[19] And while he discarded the Absolute Mind of Hegel, as also all forms of absolute idealism and *a priori* rationalism,[20] his thought continued to struggle for something to take their place. The notion of continuity of organism and environment in a single interaction supplied in part the unity that he demanded, but his thought reached out for something more. He realized that any experience is dissatisfied with the present moment, that there is in the human spirit a restlessness with existing situations. His analysis of experience led him to the theory that there are levels of unification of experience; the unification of the various elements of each

---

[17] "From Absolutism to Experimentalism," *Contemporary American Philosophy*, eds. George P. Adams and Wm. Pepperell Montague (New York: The Macmillan Company, 1930), II, 13–27. For a thorough treatment of Dewey's early espousal of and gradual break with Hegelianism, as well as of its lasting influence on his thought, see Morton G. White, *The Origin of Dewey's Instrumentalism* (New York: Columbia University Press, 1943).

[18] *Ibid.*, p. 19.

[19] *Ibid.*, pp. 20–21.

[20] *Logic: The Theory of Inquiry* (New York: Holt, Rinehart & Winston, Inc., 1938), pp. 531–534.

experience with one another, the unification of each experience with that which immediately precedes and that which immediately follows, and the unification of the total onward process of experience with an indefinite and infinite whole which gives meaning and coherence to each individual experience and to human existence in general.

But once he had advanced this far, he stopped short. His surging insights were smothered by his bias against an Absolute because, in his mind, the Absolute remained outside experience, could not be attained and separated man from nature. The notion of an imaginative projection of ideal possibilities was discussed in the previous chapter in relation to Dewey's theory of religion and religious experience. The same objection brought against it then applies here also. What is actually supposed to give meaning to human experience and to the whole of life does not exist. Nor will it ever be achieved for the individual. It is a vague and indefinite something projected into the future, always growing and developing, while the individual himself is always on the way to achieving it but never quite succeeding. The very thing which is supposed to give meaning to the present moment is not what the self *will* become but what some nameless individual or individuals *may* become. One may ask how this ideal can give satisfaction and realization to the individual. Experience will always be incomplete and truncated; forever pushing on to completion but never quite arriving.

In projecting an ideal self and an ideal Universe, Dewey had left actual contact with the existing self and the world, though he thought that some contact was still maintained through imagination and intuition. His ideal was still within nature since it arose from nature and could be achieved by interaction of the various elements in nature. Yet this imaginative projection can never fulfill the high hopes expected of it since its very vagueness and indefiniteness deprive it of the power to satisfy the longing of the human spirit for actual realization in the eventual possession of the goal of its aspirations.

And yet, in spite of its inadequacies, Dewey's sense of wholeness can provide the starting point for further development. One could recognize and accept the inner striving of the human person for self-realization on ever wider and deeper levels and allow it full expression. There is in nature a cry for fulfillment, for that which gives meaning to the highest manifestations of nature. On this point the naturalist and transcendentalist are in agreement. Where they disagree is in the object which satisfies that inner drive. The naturalist maintains that the goal must emerge from nature and remain in nature. The previous discussion has pointed out the inadequacy of such a goal.

Taking the same starting point, the transcendentalist opens himself completely to the demands of experience; not merely when it strives to unify isolated elements of a single experience, not only when it pushes beyond the present moment to link up with what is yet to come, but also when by an inner and unquenchable restlessness it seeks to transcend the limitations of a vague and indefinite goal, and strives to unite every human aspiration, especially that of love for a community of people, in a transcendent center. Consequently, the Absolute is not an impossible goal but rather the term of man's striving; it does not suddenly emerge from nowhere but arises out of the incompleteness of experience itself and is demanded by experience; it is not unintelligible and indefinite but is rather that which focuses the onward striving of human experience and gives it its only meaning and fulfillment.

The "Onward Thrust" of Experience and Nature

In the treatment of Dewey's sense of wholeness, discussion has centered around the final stage of experience, that is, satisfaction which has been achieved by prior activity. An attempt was made to show that in the sense of wholeness connected with satisfaction Dewey's thought is capable of going beyond the confines of a narrow naturalism. It will be the task of this section to show that the same may be said of the preliminary stages which lead to and terminate in satisfaction. Specifically, we wish to indicate that, while Dewey explicitly rejects finality in its traditional sense, he has not successfully done so. In the preliminary stages of experience there seems to be an inner direction, an onward thrust, both in man and in the cosmos, giving shape to the onward process of experience and nature. Man is not completely static in facing nature prior to conscious reflection nor is the cosmos neutral regarding human aims and values. In the course of our discussion it will be necessary to review some aspects of Dewey's position on ends and logic.

In his work on ends, Dewey is trying to reject what he would call two extreme positions.[21] On the one hand, he rejects "ends in nature,"

---

[21] See *Experience and Nature* (New York: W. W. Norton & Company, Inc., 1929), chap. III.

or "final causes" in the traditional Aristotelian sense where objects by an innate tendency reach a prearranged goal. On the other hand, he rejects what he calls "ends in mind," that is, conscious aims developed in individual consciousness independently of nature. This is related to his rejection of logical theories which are constructed purely in the mind without contact with contingent reality.

Dewey then proposes his theory of "ends-in-view." According to this position, ends are found neither entirely in nature nor entirely in mind, but in the interaction between the two. The inquiring subject, in confronting environing conditions, projects possible consequences to be attained by overt action. When the consequences are attained, they are conclusions and fulfillments only as they are results of prior reflection, choice and effort. In other words, nature without the inquiring subject cannot be said to be directed toward a goal. A natural end occurring without the intervention of the human subject is merely a terminus, a boundary, and does not merit any such title as end as understood in classic metaphysics.

This would seem to be a clear rejection of any directive thrust in the cosmos. But is it as clear as it seems to be? There are indications in Dewey's discussion of the logical situation which make such a clear rejection dubious. He speaks, for example, of the antecedents of logical procedure, of that which provokes thought. Actually, it is an experience, organized or constituted as a whole, which is beginning to disintegrate, to fall to pieces. It is a situation in conflict with itself. But note here that the experience, even while disintegrating, is dynamic. Of course, in its integrated stage it is dynamic, too, and that is why Dewey has described an experience as "a future implicated in a present." [22] This does not mean that the future is already contained in the present, in germ, as it were, merely awaiting the inevitable development of mechanistic laws. He was opposed to all forms of mechanistic determinism of the late nineteenth century as he was to all forms of transcendentalism. Yet neither does it mean merely that a future will somehow develop from a present situation, given time and the operation of man. Rather, the present is already on its way to becoming a future, has the tendency, drive, urge to develop.

But in its disintegrating stage, too, the experience is dynamic. The

22 "The Need for a Recovery of Philosophy," *Creative Intelligence: Essays in the Pragmatic Attitude* (New York: Holt, Rinehart & Winston, Inc., 1917), p. 12.

elements are at odds with each other, in tension against each other. Yet the incompatibility at issue is an active one; although at odds with one another, the elements are actively contending for their proper place and relationship, they are striving toward a "re-formation of the whole and to a restatement of the parts." [23]

It should be noted that the situation here described is one that precedes reflection. In other words, independently of conscious direction, the parts of the experience are in movement toward each other, a movement tending to a unified arrangement of the elements. In other words, the elements are not going nowhere, in random, haphazard movement. They are already striving to a re-integration. It is this which constitutes the thought situation.

This dynamism is also seen in Dewey's treatment of what he calls "suggestion." This refers to the initial steps taken to bring a possible solution to a given disturbed condition. In this suggestion, the mind simply "leaps forward" to a possible solution.[24]

Now notice how Dewey explains the origin of this "suggestion."

> The first suggestion occurs spontaneously; it comes to mind automatically; it springs up; it "pops," as we have said, "into the mind"; it flashes upon us. There is no direct control of its occurrence; the idea just comes or it does not come; that is all that can be said.[25]

Dewey states further that there is nothing intellectual about the occurrence of the suggestion. "The intellectual element consists in *what we do with it,* how we use it, *after* its sudden occurrence as an idea." [26] Something similar is found in a treatment which Dewey gives of "intuition." It occurs in *Art as Experience* where he is describing how a disturbed situation becomes resolved.

> "Intuition" is that meeting of the old and new in which the readjustment involved in every form of consciousness is effected suddenly by means of a quick and unexpected harmony which in its bright abruptness is like a flash of revelation; although in fact it is prepared by long and slow incubation. Oftentimes the union of old and new, of foreground and background, is accomplished only by effort, prolonged perhaps to the point of pain. In any case, the background of organized

---

[23] *Essays in Experimental Logic* (Chicago: University of Chicago Press, 1916), p. 123.

[24] *How We Think,* 2nd ed. rev. (New York: D. C. Heath & Company, 1933), p. 107.

[25] *Ibid.,* p. 109.

[26] *Ibid.*

meanings can alone convert the new situation from the obscure into the clear and luminous. When old and new jump together, like sparks when the poles are adjusted, there is intuition. This latter is thus neither an act of pure intellect in apprehending rational truth nor a Crocean grasp by spirit of its own images and states.[27]

In the above examples, one can see the directive thrust first in the environing conditions prior to reflective thought, and then in the inquiring subject once thought is under way. In a section of his *Logic: The Theory of Inquiry*, called "The Operational Character of Facts-Meanings," [28] this thrust is seen more clearly both in man and in the cosmos at the very moment when the latter are engaged in mutual interplay. First Dewey sets up the problem. In a disturbed situation, the observed facts and the proposed solution or ideational contents as expressed in ideas are related to each other in such a way that the first provides a clarification of the problem and the latter proposes a possible solution. The observed facts are already in existence while the ideational subject-matter is non-existential.

The question now arises as to how they cooperate in resolving the existing situation. If both elements are considered to be static, just facing one another, there would be no resolution of the problem. Hence, Dewey goes on to say that the only way out of the dilemma is to recognize that both observed facts and entertained ideas are operational. Regarding the ideas, he says:

> Ideas are operational in that they instigate and direct further operations of observation; they are proposals and plans for acting upon existing conditions to bring new facts to light and to organize all the selected facts into a coherent whole.[29]

Turning now to the observed facts, let us notice the terms that Dewey uses to describe the operational character of these facts. Here he has in mind more the case of an inquiry that demands a long series of operations, but it is clear that the basic points which interest us are found in any inquiry.

> When the problematic situation is such as to require extensive inquiries to effect its resolution, a series of interactions intervenes. Some observed facts point to an idea that stands for a possible solution. This idea evokes more observations. Some of the newly observed facts link

---

27 *Art as Experience*, p. 266.
28 *Logic: The Theory of Inquiry*, pp. 112–114.
29 *Ibid.*, pp. 112–113.

up with those previously observed and are such as to rule out other observed things with respect to their evidential function. The new order of facts suggests a modified idea (or hypothesis) which occasions new observations whose result again determines a new order of facts, and so on until the existing order is both unified and complete.[30]

From this analysis, it would seem that Dewey recognized both in man *and* in the rest of nature a directive striving, an onward thrust, leading both to new completions. Neither man nor the cosmos stand facing one another in neutral fashion. Each comes forward to meet the other; each takes the initiative. There is a mutual interplay such that both are changed and perfected. One is a stimulus to the other for the attainment of a higher unification. Observed facts "point" to an idea; the idea "evokes" more observations. Facts "link up" with those previously observed, the new order of facts "suggests" a modified idea "occasioning" new observations resulting in a new order of facts, "and so on until the existing order is both unified and complete." So "alive" is this mutual interplay that, if one did not know better, he would suppose that Dewey is here guilty of some sort of animism.

In any case, even independently of man, nature seems to be endowed with a directive striving. In the logical situation, the cosmos is seen to be not only not indifferent to human drives and ideals, but actively attuned to them, in the sense that by this directive striving it comes forward to meet man half way, as it were. In fact, a re-examination of Dewey's whole notion of interaction would reveal a similar tendency. For in every interaction between living beings and environment, from the lowest to the highest, there is the same interplay, the same coming forward of organism and environment in which both are altered and perfected, in which new completions come into existence, and in which both organism and environment find fulfillment of natural capacities.

Furthermore, in limiting ends to "ends-in-view" as the object of deliberate human planning and striving, Dewey has not satisfactorily explained the origin of ends. From one point of view, it may be said that he has accounted for the existence of values, ideals and ends. These have their rise in man. But, from another point of view, the problem still remains as to the origin of these in *nature*. For after all, in his view man himself is a part of nature and is subject to substantially the same conditions as the rest of nature. If the latter possesses no directive

---

[30] *Ibid.*, p. 113.

force within itself, how account for its sudden emergence in man? In addition, as seen in his treatment of the logical situation and the operational character of facts and ideas, Dewey's thought seems open to a direction in nature even independently of man.

What conclusion can be drawn from all this? At the very least it can be said that, in spite of his explicit statements, Dewey has not effectively eliminated a directive force in nature. Objectively his thought is open to any extension which may be made of this thrust, even, one might add, to an extension to a transcendental. Dewey would say, of course, that such an extension is impossible. But, at least in his analysis of ends, he has not demonstrated this impossibility.

As a final word, it may be noted that if there is any validity to the above treatment of Dewey's notion of community, his "sense of wholeness" and "onward thrust," they must be considered in any future evaluation of Dewey's naturalism. They have been largely ignored by those who would press hard the naturalistic elements of his thought, somewhat as in the past Aristotelian scholars pressed the tight, logical, deductive aspects of the Stagirite's thought and minimized passages where he is indefinite, tentative, probing, developing, even self-contradictory. It is only by opening our minds to all dimensions of a philosophy that we understand it truly and at the same time enable it to have more fruitful consequences.

From a transcendentalist's viewpoint, there is definite merit in such an approach. He has met a naturalist theory of experience on its own terms, has shown its inadequacy as well as a means of supplying for it, and has, at the same time, discovered the possibility of preserving the many valid and valuable insights of naturalism. The burden of a large portion of this book has been precisely to show that naturalism in America has pointed up real problems and has made some positive steps toward their solution. It would be a pity if these contributions were lost because of a failure on the part of the transcendentalist to appreciate the fact that the modern experience in America has manifested itself in new ways, that rather than leading to a rejection of the transcendental, the American experience can give it a new affirmation and expression enabling it to become pertinent to new problems.

VIII   CONCLUSION

In a work like the present, where a limited purpose is envisioned, much more will always remain to be said. However, it is hoped that what has herein been written will rather be a beginning—a beginning of further inquiry into the problems that John Dewey has raised. For whether one chooses to agree or disagree with him, the questions which he raises can no longer be ignored. They are the problems not merely of John Dewey, or even of a great segment of the American people; they are the problems of the world. For this reason, John Dewey must be credited with raising basic problems and with presenting seminal ideas for the solution of these problems. Hence, perhaps the best way in which to conclude this study is to set down those elements of his thought which, in the opinion of the present writer at least, are most important and promise to be most fruitful for the development of future thought in America.

Mention must first be made of Dewey's position regarding the on-going process of nature. Evolution, we know, has done much to make this concept dominant to such an extent that the world is now being considered in terms of evolution itself. Allied to this is Dewey's appreciation for the fact that experience must keep pace with the ongoing process of environing conditions if the individual is to reach self-realization on ever higher levels. It should be abundantly clear from our whole discussion on experience and human development that Dewey has pointed up something of prime importance when he emphasizes the social aspect of development on all levels and the importance of interaction between organism and environment. If he has done anything, he has shown that man cannot develop his personality, cannot achieve self-realization, without interacting with his environment. Growth in experience, and hence in fulfillment and self-realization, requires that man become an integral part of the ongoing process, that he deal with natural things and events, that he shake off his isolation which will only stunt his personality, that he strive to develop his full potentialities for the unfolding of the human person.

From this viewpoint, man's natural development demands the accompanying development of the world in which he lives. We see here a spiraling effect which is essential to Dewey's whole approach. Man develops by improving his environment; the environment as improved responds by setting up a new pattern of activity within man himself, who in turn acts upon the environment in a never-ending series. Here in all its force is Dewey's principle that when the organism and environment interact new potentialities are actualized and in the actualization both are improved.

It is important to note that the world with which man interacts in order to expand and which is improved in that interaction cannot include merely natural objects of the mineral, vegetative and animal kingdom. Dewey and others have stressed the importance of the cultural and social milieu for man's expansion. Human environment will include as an essential and primary element the human institutions which surround him, with which he interacts and which improve with him in the interaction. For this reason the cultural aspects of man's environment are the most important ones for human self-realization. If they are overlooked or even slighted, the consequences for human development will be serious. It should follow that the development of the cultural milieu is essential for any human development. For this reason, any philosophy must take seriously human progress and achievement.

All this has a definite relation to two key concepts of Dewey, namely, human creativity and self-realization. Consider, for example, the evolution of the material universe. It is striking how chaotic it once was. And despite its continued onward march over interminable periods preceding man, evolution was a long and labored process, proceeding through false starts, blind alleys and temporary reversals. But with the advent of man upon the scene, evolution became conscious of itself, and from then on the world's development moved ahead with accelerated speed. Man has made great strides in his efforts to gain control of nature so that he might more firmly and surely direct the future course of its development.

In this regard, Dewey's thought can be a great stimulus for creative thinking. One can seize with joy upon his high idealism as he envisions man as the great artist who literally fashions and creates a new world. The universe is the canvas upon which the artist paints his colors in new and exciting patterns, and in the work feels the exhilaration of expanding capacities.

It follows that philosophy, and religion too, must always keep in contact with material conditions. Man, by any standard, is not entirely an alien in the universe nor is matter entirely hostile to man. Matter is that in and through which man will reach fulfillment. The importance of matter must be taken seriously by the spiritualist and transcendentalist as well as by the naturalist, and once philosophy and religion lose contact with material conditions, they also lose contact with an essential means of achieving self-realization. Even though one should maintain that man's aspirations do not stop with matter, and that his self-development is not limited to it, such a position must come to terms with matter and show the individual how his dealings with it can be the means of achieving moral and religious development of the highest order.

If the individual does not see the relevance of matter in all its implications, if consequently he attempts to withdraw from it, he will soon give up the struggle as hopeless since it will mean a denial of those aspirations which are essential to him as a human being that feels within him the drive towards growth and development. He will then turn to matter with a vengeance because he has become discouraged in fighting a losing battle. There will result a materialism of a worse kind against which Dewey warned. The death which is here involved is the death of the human person even on the higher dimensions of religious development.

So often warnings are voiced regarding the dangers of becoming too immersed in matter. Implied in this line of reasoning seems to be the argument that if one is to go to extremes, it is better to do so in the direction of aversion to matter than of immersion in it. But this is to miss the main issue. For even the exaggeration in the direction of withdrawal from matter will ultimately result in immersion in matter. One would do well to read again the comparison which Dewey makes between transcendentalists and spiritual leaders on the one hand and sensualists and materialists on the other. In his view, the former are as bad as the latter when they obscure the relevance of matter to human self-realization and thus open up the way for a materialism of the worst kind.

Important, too, for Dewey's philosophy is his concept of "social awareness" without which man will never achieve self-realization. By this he hoped to eliminate private interest in pecuniary gain which is the cause of the "lost individual" who feels a sense of isolation because he is not involved in shared means to shared goals. Thus the sense of "social awareness" includes a solidarity of all men based on a profound respect for the dignity of the human person. In Dewey's framework, the individual is a person with capacities and potentialities that far surpass those of other natural beings in the universe, in whose hands is committed the awesome responsibility of furthering the ongoing processes of the universe and especially of man.

Applied to the worker, a sense of social awareness consists in his seeing the relation of his work to the furthering of the goods of humanity. The way in which the worker in a modern industrialized age improves the human estate is by his work which is already materially social. He must now see the connection between the work he does, which is a shared means, to the results achieved, which are the shared goals. Thus, he will see that he and his fellow workers are engaged in a community enterprise, that of furthering the ongoing process of nature, particularly of man, in a way adapted to the industrialized, technological age in which we live. This concept of social awareness attempts to integrate the experiences not only of the worker and the "common man," but also of the captains of industry, the intellectuals and the politicians. Dewey sees all of these uniting in a common cause to achieve for themselves and for mankind the highest possible experience.

In this ideal, Dewey has faced boldly and confidently those aspects of modern civilization which call for the most delicate and careful handling, namely, the scientific and technological. As Dewey has said, science is here and we must take account of it. Not only is science here in the sense that we cannot ignore it, but it is here in the sense that its onward growth is an outward manifestation of the growth going on within the individual. Science must be looked on as an ally in the process of enriching human experience.

There is one aspect of Dewey's thought to which many will take exception; his position, namely, that one can no longer work out human self-realization from the standpoint of an Absolute. Hence, the traditional notions of a transcendent God and of religion are banned from his philosophy. To proceed in this manner is to court disaster and for this reason it can be said that Dewey's philosophy and all forms of naturalism, insofar as they are committed to this position, are doomed to failure. Moreover, such a position will have tragic consequences for any system of morals, religion and human self-realization. However, though Dewey may have explicitly eliminated the transcendental, his notion of community, "sense of wholeness" and "onward thrust" are open to it and provide a starting point for anyone who would wish to extend further his insights.

Certainly Dewey has not said everything and consequently he has not had the final word. It is questionable whether this is within the competence of any man. In many respects, too, his ideas are not new for they may be found in men like Peirce, James, and Meade, to whom he acknowledged a debt. Yet, he went beyond all of these in the development of ideas and in the projection of hypotheses. Future thought in America must go beyond Dewey too, though it is difficult to see how it can avoid going through him. In this respect, one may apply to John Dewey a paraphrase of a statement made regarding Sigmund Freud:

> Whether one agrees with John Dewey's philosophy in whole or in part, or not at all, one must admit that he gave the whole of philosophical (and related) thought a new direction from which there is no return.[1]

---

[1] See General Introduction, by E. B. Strauss, to Roland Dalbiez, *Psychoanalytical Method and the Doctrine of Freud*, trans. T. F. Lindsay (New York: Longmans, Green & Co., Inc., 1941), I, v.

SELECTED BIBLIOGRAPHY

The following is a selected bibliography. A complete list of John Dewey's writings may be found in the Schilpp volume (mentioned below), pp. 611–686. Books available in paperbound editions have been noted.

Books by John Dewey

Art as Experience. New York: G. P. Putnam's Sons, 1934. Paperbound: New York: G. P. Putnam's Sons, Capricorn Books, 1958.

A Common Faith. New Haven: Yale University Press, 1934. Paperbound: New Haven: Yale University Press, 1960.

Democracy and Education. New York: The Macmillan Company, 1916. Paperbound: New York: The Macmillan Company, 1961.

Essays in Experimental Logic. Chicago: University of Chicago Press, 1916. Paperbound: New York: Dover Publications, Inc., n.d.

Ethics. 2nd ed. rev. New York: Holt, Rinehart & Winston, Inc., 1908. (With James H. Tufts.)

Experience and Education. New York: The Macmillan Company, 1939.

Experience and Nature. New York: W. W. Norton & Company, Inc., 1929. Paperbound: New York: Dover Publications, Inc., 1958.

Freedom and Culture. New York: G. P. Putnam's Sons, 1939.

How We Think. 2nd ed. rev. New York: D. C. Heath & Company, 1933.

Human Nature and Conduct. New York: Holt, Rinehart & Winston, Inc., 1922.

Individualism Old and New. New York: G. P. Putnam's Sons, 1930.

Liberalism and Social Action. New York: G. P. Putnam's Sons, 1935.

Logic: The Theory of Inquiry. New York: Holt, Rinehart & Winston, Inc., 1938.

Philosophy and Civilization. New York: G. P. Putnam's Sons, 1931.

Problems of Men. New York: Philosophical Library, Inc., 1946.

The Public and Its Problems. New York: Holt, Rinehart & Winston, Inc., 1927.

Reconstruction in Philosophy. 2nd ed. rev. Boston: The Beacon Press, 1948. (Paperbound)

The School and Society. 2nd ed. rev. Chicago: University of Chicago Press, 1915. Paperbound: The Child and the Curriculum and The School and Society. Chicago: The University of Chicago Press, Phoenix Books, 1956.

Books about John Dewey

Blewett, S. J., John (ed.), John Dewey: His Thought and Influence. New York: Fordham University Press, 1960.

Feldman, W. T., The Philosophy of John Dewey: A Critical Analysis. Baltimore: The Johns Hopkins Press, 1934.

Geiger, George R., John Dewey in Perspective. New York: Oxford University Press, 1958.

Hook, Sidney, John Dewey: An Intellectual Portrait. New York: The John Day Company, 1939.

———— (ed.), John Dewey: Philosopher of Science and Freedom. New York: The Dial Press, 1950.

Schilpp, Paul Arthur (ed.), The Philosophy of John Dewey. 2nd ed. rev. New York: The Tudor Publishing Co., 1951.

White, Morton G., The Origin of Dewey's Instrumentalism. New York: Columbia University Press, 1943.

INDEX

147

DATE DUE

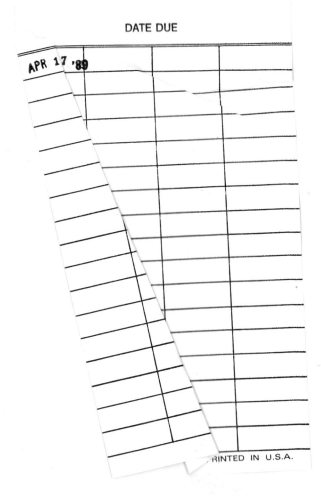

APR 17 '89

PRINTED IN U.S.A.